A. C. Clark
from
R. B. Mowat—

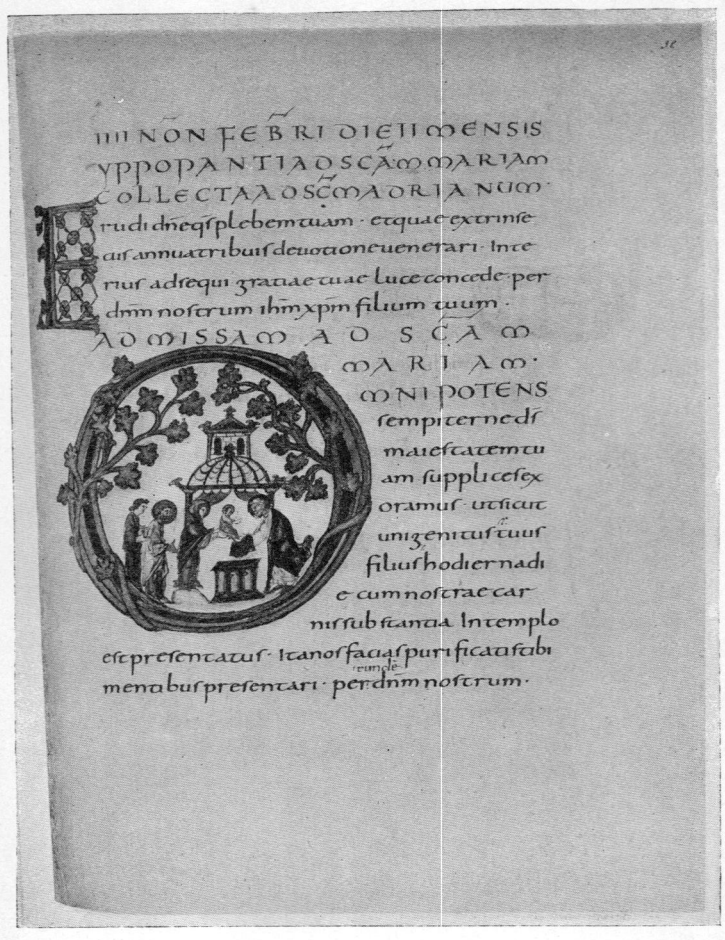

PAGE OF A CAROLINGIAN BOOK

(written for Charlemagne's son Drogo)

EINHARD'S
LIFE OF CHARLEMAGNE
THE LATIN TEXT

EDITED, WITH INTRODUCTIONS AND NOTES,

BY

H. W. GARROD

FELLOW AND TUTOR OF MERTON COLLEGE
FORMERLY ASSISTANT TUTOR OF CORPUS CHRISTI COLLEGE

AND

R. B. MOWAT

FELLOW AND ASSISTANT TUTOR OF CORPUS CHRISTI COLLEGE
OXFORD

'Unus quisque legens tanto citius spiritualiter intellegit quanto prius in litteraturae magisterio plenius instructus fuerit.'

CHARLEMAGNE.

OXFORD
AT THE CLARENDON PRESS
1915

OXFORD UNIVERSITY PRESS
LONDON   EDINBURGH   GLASGOW   NEW YORK
TORONTO   MELBOURNE   BOMBAY
HUMPHREY MILFORD M.A.
PUBLISHER TO THE UNIVERSITY

PREFACE

THE primary object of this book is to satisfy the needs of students in this University reading for the Previous Examination in Modern History. Some of these are not finished Latin scholars; and this will explain why the text has occasionally been annotated, or translated, where it would present little or no difficulty to students more familiar with Latin idiom or vocabulary.

It is hoped, however, that the book may serve to introduce to a rather wider public a work which may fairly be called the literary masterpiece of the Middle Ages.

Sections I–IV of the Introduction, together with the Text and the Notes upon the Prologues and chapters i–xi, xxi–xxvi, are the work of Mr. Garrod. Mr. Mowat is responsible for Section V of the Introduction, and for the Notes upon chapters xii–xx, xxvii–xxxiii. But either editor has revised the work of the other.

In the preparation of the Text we owe much to the edition of Waitz (Waitz-Holder-Egger). In the Notes and Introductions we have tried to follow mediaeval rather than modern authorities. But among modern books of which we have made use should be mentioned : Richter's *Zeittafeln der deutschen Geschichte im Mittelalter* ; Lavisse's *Histoire de France,* ii. 1 ; Ranke's *Kritik fränkisch-deutscher Reichsannalisten* ; Waitz's *Deutsche Verfassungsgeschichte* iii ; the Lives of Charlemagne by Dr. Hodgkin and Mr. H. W. C. Davis ; and Hodgkin's *Italy and her Invaders,* vii and viii. In Section IV of the Introduction, and occasionally in the Notes, Traube's *Einleitung in die lateinische Philologie des Mittelalters* has been helpful.

The Editors are much indebted to Mr. H. W. C. Davis who read this volume in proof and made valuable suggestions. They have also to thank the Committee of the New Palaeographical Society for permission to reproduce the facsimile which forms the frontispiece.

The Editors have throughout elected to speak of 'Charlemagne', and not of 'Charles the Great'—to follow, that is, a tradition sanctioned by Milton and by Gibbon rather than a fashion certainly new and probably pedantic. They hope that they may be acquitted of any sinister design to obscure the essentially Teutonic character of the life and actions of Charlemagne.

H. W. G.
R. B. M.

OXFORD, *February* 1915.

CONTENTS

	PAGE
THE TEXT OF THE *VITA KAROLI*	vii
INTRODUCTION	xiii
I. Einhard	xiii
II. The Good Faith of Einhard	xv
III. Other Authorities for the Life of Charlemagne	xxx
IV. German Culture in the Early Middle Ages	xxxii
V. The Carolingian Empire: its Limits and Administration	xlii
TEXT	1
NOTES	39
Index of Places and Peoples	79
Index of Personal Names	81

ILLUSTRATIONS

PAGE OF A CAROLINGIAN BOOK . . *Frontispiece*

THE EMPIRE OF CHARLEMAGNE . . . *at end*

THE TEXT OF THE *VITA KAROLI*

THE *Vita Karoli* has been preserved to us in more than eighty MSS., of which no less than sixty were employed by G. H. Pertz, in his edition of 1829 (*Mon. Germ. Hist.*, *SS.*, ii, pp. 443 sqq.). Pertz's Apparatus Criticus is a magnificent monument of that kind of industry which, seeking no end save itself, conceives itself to have infinite rights and almost no duties. Its merciless prolixity called forth the sharp animadversion of P. Jaffé, who, in 1867, sweeping aside the whole of Pertz's sixty MSS., produced a text based upon a single authority, the excellent Paris MS., which he has the merit to have discovered (*Bibl. Rer. Germ.* iv, pp. 487 sqq.). In 1880 appeared the edition of Pertz-Waitz (now Pertz-Waitz-Holder-Egger, Hanover and Leipsic, 1911). Waitz employs some twenty MSS., most of them used already by Pertz, and some of them too hastily set aside by Jaffé. But his twenty MSS. end by being almost as tiresome as the sixty of Pertz. In one respect they are more so— he employs for them a notation so complicated that his Apparatus is barely intelligible. Each MS. is denoted by at least two symbols, and a fair number by as many as three (e.g. $A3^a$, $B3^b$, &c.). The revision of Waitz by Holder-Egger adds little and takes nothing away.

Waitz managed to persuade himself that the text of the *Vita* had become deeply depraved in the short interval between the date at which the work was composed and that at which our earliest MSS. of it were written (p. xvii, 1911). It is true that there is a good deal of depraved spelling. It is true that we have many MSS. written by scribes who were careless, or ignorant, or both. It is also true that in one or two passages we have some reason to suspect trivial interpolations. Yet on the whole it would be hard to find a work dating from so early a period where we had so little room to doubt what the author himself wrote. And a proof of it is this: that between the edition of Jaffé, based on a single MS., and that of Waitz, based on twenty, there is really no important difference. The fact is that there are at least half a dozen MSS. of the *Vita*, written within fifty years of Einhard's death, any one of which would, with a revised orthography, furnish an excellent working text.

Waitz divides the MSS. into three classes, which he calls *ABC*. The following facts supply the principle of this threefold classification:

(1) The MSS. of Classes *A* and *B* lack the Preface to the *Vita*;

(2) The last two sentences in chap. xix are found in MSS. of the *A* and *B* Classes, but are absent from MSS. of the *C* Class;

(3) At chap. xviii, lines 22–3, the *C* Class MSS. have a whole clause not found in the texts of the other two classes (and offer *quattuor* for *tres*);

(4) The MSS. of Class *B* differ from those of both the *A* and the *C* Class by a striking omission in chap. ix, *fin*. They want there the clause in which the death of Roland is mentioned;

(5) The *B* Class MSS. append to the *Vita* six elegiac couplets in honour of Einhard, written by one Gerwardus, Librarian to Charlemagne and to Louis the Pious.[1]

These facts undoubtedly point to the conclusion that all our MSS. are derived from three distinct copies, made some time in the early part of the ninth century. Our ideal should clearly be to restore, by a comparison of the readings of the MSS. of each class, the three lost copies that lie behind our texts. The pursuit of this ideal is the *raison d'être* of Waitz's text, and affords the explanation of the extraordinary system of notation which he employs. But Waitz must be said to perish in the pursuit of an ideal which is, frankly, unattainable. The three classes

[1] The verses are as follows:—
> Hos tibi versiculos ad laudem, maxime princeps,
>   edidit aeternam memoriamque tuam
> Gerwardus supplex famulus, qui mente benigna
>   egregium extollit nomen ad astra tuum.
> hanc, prudens, gestam noris tu scribere, lector,
>   Einhardum magni magnificum Karoli.

which he establishes—and they are real enough—have already, even in our earliest codices—become infinitely 'contaminated'; that is to say, the MSS. of each class have fused the tradition of their own with that of the other two classes. One or two MSS. of the *A* Class *have* the Preface, deriving it, no doubt, from some MS. of the *C* Class. Some MSS. of the *C* Class *have* the last sentences of chap. xix. Some MSS. of the *B* Class have *not* the verses of Gerwardus, or have only a part of them. Yet more serious is the fact that, where we are confronted with variant lections, it very rarely happens that the same reading is found in all, or even most, of the MSS. which are of the same Class. There is endless cross-division. It may be said, in fact, that the five considerations, noted above, which enable us to discern a three-fold grouping of MSS., fail to carry us very much beyond themselves. Einhard's work must have been endlessly transcribed, from the time of its first publication; and its numerous transcribers have, as it were, conspired together to obliterate the distinctions between the different classes of MSS.

This being so, an elaborate array of MSS., like that of Waitz, serves no real purpose. Indeed, his vast collection of variants rather obscures than illustrates the cognation of the MSS. We need an *Apparatus Criticus* which shall take a middle course between Waitz and Jaffé, just as Waitz endeavoured to take a middle course between Pertz and Jaffé. Among the twenty MSS. employed in the last edition of Waitz two are clearly much superior to any others. These are, firstly, the Paris MS.10758, of the ninth or tenth century—the MS. used by Jaffé, called in this edition *C*; and, secondly, the Vienna MS., *Bibl. Pal.* 510, written in the ninth century, called in this edition *A*. (This MS. lacks chap. i, *Gens Meroingorum* to *et eam per*(*parvi*), line 18, as well as chap. ix, *impedimentorum*, line 13, to chap. xi, *filia*, line 4; both losses have been repaired by a scribe of the twelfth century.) Each of these MSS. is easily the best representative of the class to which it belongs—*A* represents Waitz's *A* Class, *C* represents Waitz's *C* Class, in a manner much more satisfactory than those classes would be represented if we cited the readings of the other MSS. Of Waitz's third class no single MS. is even a tolerable representative, nor, taken together, would the MSS. of this class furnish anything save a very faulty text. Whether this Class has any critical value at all is a question the answer to which depends entirely on the view which may be taken of the genuineness of the clause in chap. ix which refers to Roland. If that clause be a later insertion, then the *B* Class are clearly not negligible. We have no clear means of determining this question; and it has been thought better, therefore, in this edition, to take some account of MSS. of the *B* Class. That Class is, accordingly, represented by two of its MSS., which seem, on the whole, less faulty than the others. One of these, called here *B*, is the Montpellier MS. 360, of the ninth or tenth century, as collated by Waitz. The other is a Vienna MS., *Bibl. Pal.* 473, saec. x. It contains only chap. xviii, *ceteraque*, line 4, to the end. It is cited in our *Apparatus* as *b*. These two MSS. will, if they serve no other purpose—and we are not clear that they do—show clearly the inferior character of the tradition of their class. This inferiority is the more noteworthy because we might well have hoped a good deal from a class of MSS. which, preserving, as it does, the verses of Gerwardus, might have been supposed to go back to some copy of the *Vita* preserved in the Library of Louis the Pious. But the Royal Library at Aachen certainly never contained—unless Gerwardus was a very incompetent Librarian—a book so badly copied as must have been the parent of the *B* Class. Gerward seems to have been a personal friend of Einhard (see *Epp. Einh.* 52, Duemmler, *Epp. Kar. Aev.* iii, p. 135); and it is possible that he may have possessed a copy of the work somewhat carelessly made for private use—what we should call, in publishing, an 'advance copy'. Such a copy might very well lack Einhard's Preface, as do both the *A* and *B* Classes.

The Prologue of Walafrid is found only in three fifteenth-century MSS. of the *B* Class. It is printed in this edition according to B. de Simson's collation of the Freiburg (Breisgau) MS. 468. The orthography has been tacitly amended; and in the following places variants have been adopted from either of the other two MSS. :—

Line 3 *palatinos* (for *palatinus*) ; 17 *philosopharentur* (for *philosopharent*) ; 39 *ignoret* (for *ignorat*) ; 40 *praecipuam* (for *praecipuum*) ; 41 *Strabo* (for *scriba*). Otherwise, we have adhered to the Freiburg MS. throughout.

The three copies from which all our MSS. are descended were almost certainly written in Germany, and in areas, it seems probable, where—as at Fulda—Anglo-Saxon influence was strongly felt. This is the natural inference from such an error as *autem* for *enim* in chap. xix, line 24, and from such spellings as *tonicam, peccuniam, occeani, incolomis, rennuendum, aborebat, dissertissimis, excelentissimi, Pectavium, lacescebant, cominatus*, etc. : see Hellmann, *Sedulius Scottus*, pp. 118 sqq. It is in conformity with this hypothesis of Anglo-Saxon influence that we have printed throughout such forms as *Norđmanni* (attested only occasionally by our MSS.). It should be noted that in places in our text where we have merely corrected a trivial error of spelling, the reading of the MSS. is given in the *Apparatus Criticus*, but it has not been thought worth while to indicate the source of the correction.

INTRODUCTION

I

EINHARD

THE *Vita Karoli Magni* was written at some date between the years 814 and 821—Charlemagne died in 814, and we know that by 821 a copy of Einhard's work had already found a place in the Library of the monastery of Sindleozes-Auva. Einhard [1] was born at Moingewi, a village of eastern Frankland, about the year 770. He was sent to school in the neighbouring monastery of Fulda, then under the sway of the Abbot Baugulfus. Here he remained until 791, when he was admitted to the 'Palace School' of Charlemagne. The Palace School, the centre from which radiated the educational reforms which we may still, perhaps, with Gibbon, regard as constituting the noblest part of Charlemagne's glory, had been for eight years directed and informed by the learning and enthusiasm of the great Alcuin. Alcuin was an Englishman, and Fulda (founded by Boniface) was a centre of English literary activity. It was, perhaps, to the connexion of Fulda with English scholarship that Einhard owed his promotion to the Palace School. Alcuin speaks of him in a letter to Charlemagne as 'Beseleel, vester immo et noster familiaris adiutor' (*Epp.* 172, p. 283, Duemmler). The reference

---

[1] He is often referred to incorrectly as Eginhard. But this form of the name (Eginhardus, Agenardus) has no authority outside late and inferior MSS.

in the name Beseleel is to a proficiency which probably was as useful in recommending Einhard to Charlemagne as were his literary merits. Einhard, like Bezaleel of old, was skilled ' to devise cunning works, to work in gold, and in silver, and in brass, and in cutting of stones for setting, and in carving of wood ' (Exod. xxxi. 4–5). He no doubt assisted in the adornment of many of the architectural works which Charlemagne undertook, among them of the Cathedral to which Aix-la-Chapelle owes its name. Einhard speaks of himself as living ' in unbroken friendship with Charles himself and his children' (Praef. *Vit. Karl.*). It is said that it was upon Einhard's advice that in 813 Charlemagne adopted as consort in the empire his son and successor Louis the Pious. On the death of Charlemagne Einhard continued to live under the imperial favour. Louis showered upon him abbacies and estates, and between these and the Palace School Einhard divided his time until the year 830, when, unhappy amid the plots and factions which assailed his master, he sought and obtained his dismissal from court, retiring to Mulinheim (one of the properties bestowed upon him by Louis fifteen years previously). Mulinheim is now called Seligenstadt, ' the city of the Saints.' To Mulinheim Einhard carried the relics of S. Marcellinus and S. Peter. These relics were the source of many miracles, and these miracles the theme of a still extant work of Einhard, the *Translatio SS. Marcellini et Petri*, written in 830. Six years later Einhard composed another work, which we still possess, the *Libellus de adoranda Cruce*, dedicated to Servatus Lupus, subsequently famous as Abbot of Ferrières, and a scholar whose enthusiasm and many-sided activity place him on a level with the great heroes of fifteenth-century Humanism.

THE GOOD FAITH OF EINHARD

this charge first in so far as it affects the public career of Charlemagne.

There are three conjunctures in the public career of Charlemagne at which he seems especially exposed to criticism. These concern his relations (1) to his brother Carloman; (2) to Didier, king of the Lombards; (3) to Tassilo, duke of Bavaria. In each connexion the narrative of Einhard is less full than we could have wished, and seems to justify some suspicion of his motives. We will take first the case of Carloman.

The world is always kindly disposed towards dispossessed younger brothers; and it is not unnatural that Carloman should have found friends and champions. No one supposes that Einhard has said all that there is to be said for Carloman, and indeed it would be hardly reasonable to expect it from him. But what excites some suspicion against him is not that he does not state a case for Carloman, but that he does not state one for Charlemagne. That there were serious and open differences between the two brothers is certain—it is sufficiently clear from the letter addressed to them by Pope Stephen (*Codex Carolinus*, 46, p. 155, Jaffé). If the fault lay with Carloman, it was natural for Einhard to specify it. He does, indeed, in chap. xviii, charge Carloman vaguely with creating 'simultates et invidiam'—unpleasantnesses which he tells us, no doubt truly, that Charlemagne endured with singular equanimity. But no definite charge of any kind is preferred. It is usually supposed that the quarrel began in the refusal of Carloman to assist his brother in Aquitaine in 769. About this two things may be said: (1) This refusal appears in Einhard's account rather as a result than as a cause of the quarrel (chap. v, *init.*); (2) There are indications that this incident was not altogether of the character

THE GOOD FAITH OF EINHARD

must not lightly regard every practitioner in this species as self-condemned. Our judgement of Einhard should be the more circumspect in proportion as we are judging, in every criticism which we pass upon him, one of the supreme figures of history—Charlemagne himself; and we are necessarily judging either on evidence very defective and by a defective method. The defect of method proceeds partly from the defect of evidence and partly from a weakness of human nature—in connecting facts which our records present in disconnexion we can never wholly free ourselves from some uncertified preconception of the motives which ordinarily govern political and moral action. We need to remind ourselves that the diplomacy of kings is often more accidental than it appears, and that we have not yet exhausted in our ethical catalogues the possible contradictions in human nature.

Deliberate falsehood is not, we may take it, alleged against Einhard. His art is not mendacity, but a talent for *suppressio veri*. This talent, it may be said in passing, is one which Einhard, if he has it, certainly shares with the chroniclers of the time. The *Lorsch Annals*—our most complete record of the events of Charlemagne's reign—are highly disingenuous: we can often detect the omissions of their partial historian by comparison with the amplification of the work sometimes attributed to Einhard himself, the so-called *Annals of Einhard*. Being, as they are, annalistic in form, the *Lorsch Annals* can less easily cover up, or excuse, their omissions than can Einhard; and it is alleged against the author of the *Vita* that in his account, not only of the private life, but also of the political actions of his master, he has failed to put before his readers facts, or considerations, which could hardly have escaped his memory. Let us consider

Four years after the composition of this work Einhard died (March 14, 840). Not so commanding a figure in the history of the Carolingian Revival as Alcuin or, later, Lupus, Einhard has none the less in his *Life of Charlemagne* bequeathed to the world a work valuable both to the historian and to the student of literature : a work which reproduces, to a degree very remarkable in the period to which it belongs, at once the technique and the spirit of antiquity. It is a rare coincidence which has attached the epithet ' Great ' not only to the subject, but also to the author, of this slender biography. To his contemporaries, Einhard was ' Einhardus *Magnus* '. In person he was of almost dwarfish stature ; but his friends were never tired of contrasting playfully the diminutive body with the great soul which informed it. ' Tiny Nard ' (Nardus, Nardulus), Alcuin calls him— and admonishes the reader, by a rather poor jest, that ' nard, in however small a quantity, throws its sweet scent far and wide '. The same epigram points, by two rather prettier figures, the same lesson : ' The bee has a tiny frame, but it bears honey. The eye is a small member, but it rules a living body with imperial sway. Even so doth Nardulus rule his house. Reader, as you go your way, cry, "Nardulus, little Nardulus, all hail to thee!"'

II

THE GOOD FAITH OF EINHARD

Einhard's editor Walafrid claims for his author that, while praising Charlemagne, he has satisfied the critical conscience of his readers. Einhard himself, in the Preface to his work, seems mainly occupied with the thought of the gratitude which he owes to his master.

He says, however, that he has taken pains to omit nothing ' which could have come to his knowledge '. The things which ' come to our knowledge ' are commonly those which we take the pains to fetch there; and it is not difficult, even for a tolerably honest man, to avoid knowing facts which it would be impolitic, or ungrateful, to relate. The scholars of Charlemagne's Palace School were often men of the world as well as scholars. Alcuin, the presiding genius of the School, was such a man; and it is not improbable that his ' friend and helper ',[1] Einhard, resembled him. The type was one which, for obvious reasons, Charlemagne admired genuinely. It must, further, be remembered that, when Einhard wrote his *Life of Charlemagne*, he was still living upon the bounty of Charlemagne's son. To what extent can we trust either his judgement or his narrative of facts?

It may be said at once that both his style and method lend themselves easily to a presentation of history and character which, without deliberate falsification, can accommodate facts to predilections. He has taken for his model Suetonius.[2] In doing so he has freed himself from the limitations of the annalistic method, that plague of contemporary history, and achieved not only a delightful *literary* liberty, but also the freedom to look at great events through gaps which he creates in the retrospect at his own pleasure. He emphasizes his anxiety to be brief; and his method and style made it possible for him, if he wished to do so, to avoid very often, in one and the same manœuvre, prolixity and some awkward fact. Familiar History, in fact, furnishes infinite opportunity to the disingenuous, though we

[1] Alcuin, *Epp.* 172, p. 283, Duemmler.

[2] Fulda, where Einhard was educated, possessed what was probably the only MS. of Suetonius' *Lives* which then existed.

THE GOOD FAITH OF EINHARD

supposed by Einhard's version of it. Two of our annalists actually go so far as to represent the subjugation of Aquitaine as an enterprise undertaken and carried through by a co-operation of the two brothers: see note on chap. v, *init*. In the *Lorsch Annals*, again, we are given to understand that the affair in Aquitaine was trivial—Charlemagne 'cum Francorum paucis' quickly made an end of the conspiracy: he then had a meeting with his brother at Duasdives, after which ' Carlomannus se revertendo Franciam iter arripiens . . . ivit ', while Charlemagne fortified Fronsac and sent an embassy to Loup. In this account there is no suggestion of any behaviour on the part of Carloman either false or unfriendly. That suggestion comes in with the reviser and continuator of these Annals, supposed to be Einhard. The *Lorsch Annals*, in their first form, imply that all difficulty was practically at an end when the meeting at Duasdives took place. It is further to be observed that even the *Vita Karoli* does not say that Carloman refused to help Charlemagne, but rather that he promised help, which he subsequently failed to send (chap. v. 1). It is, we think, probable that the brothers had concerted some joint action: that Charlemagne was ready first: that finding his task nothing like so formidable as had been supposed he struck without waiting for his brother. Such a view reconciles all existing accounts, and it is easy to see how Carloman's failure to participate in the Aquitanian action may have given a handle to malice.

In chap. iii we are told that Carloman was surrounded by bad advisers, who wished to make an end of the system of divided kingship, and even to bring about a fratricidal war. Here three comments suggest themselves: (1) Einhard goes out of his way, when he tells us this, to assure us that there was no real danger to be apprehended from these plots—it was merely that suspicion was engendered: (2) We know no more of the advisers of Carloman than Einhard tells us. We do know, however, that among the principal persons at his court there were at least four who were there in the interests of Charlemagne, and who were instrumental in securing the succession to Charlemagne the moment that Carloman was dead (they were Wilcharius, bishop of Sitten, Folradus, the king's chaplain, and the two counts Warinus and Adalhard, *Ann. Lauriss.* a. 771, p. 148, Pertz). These agents bear a sinister look. It is difficult not to believe that Charlemagne had cast eyes on his brother's possessions, and had matured his plans, some time before Carloman died. It was, after all, the Frankish way. Pepin and the elder Carloman swiftly rid themselves of Grifo; and one has an uneasy suspicion that the elder Carloman did not retire to his monastery (chap. ii. 15 sqq.) save to the great relief—and perhaps on the soft suggestion—of Pepin; (3) The only overtures of friendship which we know Charlemagne to have made to his brother (those made through Queen Bertha) the brother seems to have received most willingly. Of this 'reconciliation' Einhard tells us nothing. His silence here may be wholly innocent. But it has been suggested that there were circumstances connected with the 'reconciliation' which made it impolitic to mention the subject at all. Of these circumstances the most noteworthy are the alliances formed by Charlemagne, in the early years of his reign, with Didier and Tassilo. The train of events is conceived to be something of this sort.

To protect himself, or to strengthen himself, against Carloman, Charlemagne entered into an alliance with both the Lombards and the Bavarians. Then, not feeling very secure as to the fidelity of these two allies, he ' reconciled ' himself with his brother. But immediately, conceiving the same mistrust of his brother as he had felt of Didier and Tassilo, he proceeded, with consummate duplicity, to enter into new engagements with the Lombard king.

Such is the reconstruction of events accepted by a recent historian of Charlemagne, who is one of his most discerning admirers. Our records here are very imperfect, and in particular the chronology of events is highly uncertain. All that we know of the Bavarian alliance is derived from an uninforming reference to it in chap. xxii of the *Life of St. Sturm* (written by a Bavarian, it may be noticed). There the alliance is dated in one of our MSS. very vaguely by the words ' illis temporibus ', and in another as falling in the fourth year of Charlemagne's reign (i. e. after the death of Carloman). Again, there is nothing to show that the arrangement with Didier was directed against, or not participated in by, Carloman. We may be content, perhaps, where so much is doubtful, to give Charlemagne some benefit of our reasonable doubts; and at least to suspend our judgement on the silence here of his biographer.

Einhard's want of fullness, or of frankness, in narrating the circumstances under which Charlemagne came into connexion with Didier is some embarrassment to him when, at the beginning of chap. vi, he has to narrate the causes of Charlemagne's first expedition into Italy. The events preceding that expedition were, briefly, these: Charlemagne had allied himself, as already noticed—and from whatever motives—with Didier and the Lombards. He cemented this alliance, or some new alliance, by marrying Didier's daughter. This marriage gave grave offence to the Pope, and it was presently to give still graver—and juster—offence to Didier : for Charlemagne almost immediately divorced his wife. On the death of Carloman in 771, Didier gave a refuge to his widow and children, and endeavoured to induce the Pope to crown the latter. When the Pope refused, Didier made war upon him. The Pope appealed to Charlemagne for assistance, and Charlemagne invaded and overthrew the Lombard kingdom. All that Einhard tells us of the causes of this Lombard war is that Charlemagne undertook it at the urgent entreaty of the Pope. He does not tell us that Charlemagne had by his alliance with Didier, exposed the Papal power to the peril of which it stood in perpetual fear, Lombard aggression, a peril from which as a Frankish king, he had a hereditary obligation to protect the Roman see. He does not tell us that Charlemagne had a quarrel of his own with Didier, nor that in that quarrel, though Didier was perhaps not altogether guiltless, Charlemagne was, to say no worse, deeply to blame. A little candour here on the part of Einhard might perhaps have assisted us in forming a judgement of Charlemagne's behaviour more gentle than seems, with the material at our disposal, possible.

The relations of Charlemagne to Duke Tassilo are rather more obscure than are his relations with Didier. While Carloman was still alive, Charlemagne had already perhaps treated Tassilo in a fashion not particularly straightforward. It is thought by many that even at this early period Charlemagne had destined the duke for the fate which overtook him twenty years later. The possession of Bavaria was important for the security of the Frankish kingdom. But it is hardly possible to determine what degree of far-sighted policy may, or may not, be presumed in Charlemagne's early period. It is conceivable that the guilt of Tassilo was real—as well as convenient ; though even among Charlemagne's supporters there were not wanting persons who were very sceptical about it. For the invasion of Bavaria in 787 Einhard (chap. xi) assigns two causes : (1) the complicity of Tassilo in the plot to restore the Lombard kingdom, (2) the alliance of Tassilo with the Avars. The first of these two charges is probable enough, though Tassilo had sufficient belief in his cause to submit it to the Pope— a little less faith in the Pope would have served his turn better. The second charge also may be true, though it seems to have its source in Bavarian malcontents. An alliance with the Avars was an undoubted treason toward Christian Europe. What has to be observed in Einhard's account of the matter is this : he appears to make the alliance with the Avars a reason for the expedition of 787. According to other authorities[1] it was a result, not a cause, of the expedition. The alliance was, in fact, made in 788, after Charlemagne had already humiliated Tassilo. Einhard's language is—perhaps intentionally—vague. But there can be no doubt that he *implies* a version of the causes of the Bavarian War which presents Tassilo's conduct in a more odious light than that in which other versions set it.

In respect to two other incidents of Charlemagne's public life, the candour of his biographer has been called in question. It has been remarked that the disaster which befel Charlemagne's forces at Roncesvalles is passed over more lightly than the issues involved made desirable ; nor has Einhard thought it worth while to instruct his readers in the futility of the adventure into Spain as a whole. It must be remembered, however, that Roncesvalles looms larger in the imagination of the modern historian than it need ; and it must

[1] See e. g. the *Lorsch Annals*—which are here particularly full.

also be remembered that the brevity here of Einhard's account involves no moral issue—it is one thing to cover up a misfortune, another to palliate criminal ambition and its constant concomitant, shabby diplomacy.[1] Whether it is by accident or design that he has failed to instruct his readers that the Christian king Charlemagne was in this expedition leagued with Saracens, is a question which we have no obvious means of determining. The other incident, in connexion with which there is some doubt whether Einhard might not have let us see more than he has, is that of Charlemagne's coronation. The difficulty has been endlessly discussed, nor need it be raised anew here. Design and accident, it is worth repeating, are so inextricably mixed in a career which grows from so complex a character as that of Charlemagne that it must sometimes have been difficult not merely for his biographer, but for the king himself, to distinguish between plot and the play of circumstance.

Some of the public actions of Charlemagne are disfigured by a vice which, while in some degree it was a vice of the time, appears in him to a degree beyond what even the custom of the Middle Ages can excuse—cruelty. The utter disappearance of Carloman's widow and children is a sinister episode. On this episode Einhard is wholly silent, and we have to draw our conclusions from our general conception of Charlemagne's character. But we can scarcely acquit Einhard of a certain disingenuousness when he goes out of his way, in speaking of the flight of these unhappy persons to Italy (chap. iii, *fin.*), to tell us that the queen had no cause at all to fear her brother-in-law. The fate, whatever it was—and it was known to Einhard—which ultimately overtook herself and her children sufficiently justifies her

[1] The *Lorsch Annals* have no reference to Roncesvalles.

prudence, and refutes her historian. Einhard appears, again, to employ an intentional vagueness when he refers to the fate which overtook Charlemagne's father-in-law, Didier. He speaks casually of ' exile ', and the unhappy king seems to have been still alive in 787 (chap. xi). He probably found a perpetual prison in some French monastery. Charlemagne, as Dr. Hodgkin remarks, ' highly valued—for his enemies—the opportunities for meditation and prayer afforded by the monotonous seclusion of the cloister '.

Charlemagne's cruelty in war is certainly not concealed from us by Einhard—though he omits, it is true, to say anything of the Massacre of Verden. The account, in chap. viii, of the subjugation of the Saxons, and, again, in chap. xiii, of the conquest of the Avars, is sufficiently frank. For Einhard's reputation one could wish it less so. He perhaps shared something of that religious enthusiasm, which is probably the deepest motive in the character and actions of his master—the enthusiasm which baptizes children in the blood of their fathers, and takes a peculiar pleasure in introducing the heathen to the bosom of the Church at the point of the sword.

The private life of Charlemagne was probably as well known to Einhard as to any man in Europe. The numerous wives and concubines of the king (though sometimes Einhard forgets the name of some one of the latter) are catalogued in chap. xviii. ' Of Charlemagne's virtues chastity ', as Gibbon says, ' was not the most conspicuous.' We may allow a good deal here to the manners of the time, and something to what peoples seem to expect from their princes ; and Einhard's catalogue will not excite surprise. Only at one or two points can we accuse his frankness. He tells us that he has no notion why Charlemagne divorced Desirée at the end of a single year. Charlemagne was tired of her; and he wanted to marry Hildegard—that is the whole rather heartless story. Of another of Charlemagne's wives, Fastrada, Einhard gives an account not entirely convincing. The cruelty of her disposition is assigned as the cause of the Thuringian conspiracy of 785-6, and of the rebellion of Pippin the Hunchback in 792. We are told that, from undue conjugal affection, Charlemagne was led ' to stray an immense distance from his natural goodness of heart and from his accustomed clemency '. We have seen something already of the ' accustomed clemency ' of Charlemagne ; and we must hesitate to put too much trust in a historian who tries to throw the blame for Charlemagne's excesses on a wife from whom, whatever her ferocity, her husband had little here to learn. After all, the most cruel act of Charlemagne's life, the massacre of 4,500 Saxons, was prior to his marriage with Fastrada.

In the matter of his wives and concubines, Charlemagne's conduct, however little defensible morally, is at least intelligible. It is less easy to understand that part of his domestic life which touches his daughters. No one of them was allowed to marry. Even Einhard confesses himself perplexed here. Charlemagne, he tells us, ' used to say that he could not do without their company ' (chap. xix). One suspects that Charlemagne spoke with grim humour—a king who so quickly got rid of his wives was likely to become proportionately tired of his daughters. And he had some reason for wishing to settle them in life. Not allowed to go far, and marry, they fared worse, and became a scandal to the court. There is no reason to credit a late legend which connects the name of Einhard with one of Charlemagne's profligate daughters. But it is noticeable that in that section where Einhard speaks of the king's daughters, there in no mention of any scandal in connexion with them save in two sentences which are not to be found in our best MS. When we remember Einhard's occasional inspirations of silence elsewhere, we shall perhaps be right in supposing that these two sentences are from the pen of some rather later, and more ingenuous, writer. Charlemagne's treatment of his daughters may probably be explained in two ways: (1) He regarded them as *permanent possibilities of political alliance*. He kept them at home in order that any one of them might be ready at any moment to seal a new diplomatic engagement. Marriages were actually arranged for two of them—in exchange for political alliances. That they all of them died single is to be attributed to the genius which Charlemagne possessed for dropping alliances which some sudden change in the political situation rendered no longer necessary to him; (2) The Frankish nobles, or the dependent dukes of the Frankish empire, were the persons among whom Charlemagne might most naturally have thought to find husbands for his daughters. But by making any one of them his son-in-law he was probably sensible that he would elevate a potential usurper, while at the same time alienating those noble suitors whom he passed by.

The Suetonian style and method, which we have already spoken of as the most notable external characteristic of Einhard's work, is especially marked in the sections dealing with Charlemagne's private life (if we except chap. xviii). So closely does Einhard reproduce, in these sections, not only the manner but the matter, not only the general style but the diction, in detail, of Suetonius, that critics have been obliged to ask themselves whether, in following Suetonius so slavishly, he has not impaired the value of his work as history: whether in fact, in his dependence upon his Latin model, he has not been led to attribute to Charlemagne qualities and accomplishments, not only moral and intellectual, but even physical, which did not characterize him: whether he has not made the founder of the Holy Roman Empire a great deal more like the founder of the Ancient Roman Empire than the facts would warrant.[1] We have here a literary problem requiring for its proper solution some tact and delicacy—the question is not one merely for the historian, but involves the whole psychology of imitative literature. A few general considerations must suffice, which may afford broad principles of guidance. It may be said safely that Einhard, whatever his defects, possessed genuine literary talent. Closely as he models his style and diction on Suetonius, he is never a clumsy imitator. We may dismiss as idle the notion that his vocabulary of pure Latin was so limited that in describing the eyes, or neck, or hair, of Charlemagne, he had to accommodate them to those of some Roman emperor portrayed by Suetonius. We must rather conceive of him as a writer so deeply saturated in Suetonius that he instinctively put the results of his own personal observation into the phrases to which his reading had habituated him. It must be remembered that Suetonius often imitates himself almost as closely as he is imitated by Einhard. His descriptions of the personal appearance and habits of

[1] The material for a discussion of the question is collected in Jaffé's note at p. 501 of the *B. R. G.* vol. iv. See also Hodgkin, *Italy and her Invaders*, viii. 127, and Davis, p. 237. Mr. Davis refers to Rudolf's use of Tacitus. We may compare also the manner in which Rahewin employs Sallust and Hegesippus in his descriptions of Barbarossa's battles.

different emperors repeat one another in phraseology—where the characteristics of one emperor happen to recur in another. Suetonius, in fact, uses 'Suetonian tags' almost as much as Einhard. It should also be noticed—as writers have already noticed—that though Einhard's chief model is the Life of Augustus, others of the Suetonian *Lives* are laid under frequent contribution. In the strange gallery of portentous kings presented in the *Vitae Caesarum* Einhard could find, if his own vocabulary failed him, words for almost any peculiarity of human habit or occupation. Still employing the phrases of Suetonius, he could, if he had wished it, have given us a very different portrait of Charlemagne. The influence of Suetonius is, in fact, a good deal more subtle and elusive than the criticisms which we have here been answering presume. In a more subtle fashion it is probable that Einhard's close dependence on Suetonius *may* have led him to give a false colour here and there to his picture of his hero. Einhard's two most attractive qualities are, when all is said, a generous love of Charlemagne and a genuine enthusiasm for antiquity. He would tend naturally to look upon his master with eyes which, habituated to the contemplation of ancient greatness, were apt to see in him the reflection of that greatness. It is likely enough that he was over-anxious to find resemblances between Charlemagne and Augustus where such resemblances were either very remote, or even non-existent. His picture of Charlemagne's habits and disposition, where it differs from other pictures, seems to differ from them precisely in those respects in which it agrees most with the Suetonian portrait of Augustus. We miss, in particular, some of those characteristics, or supposed characteristics, of Charlemagne, which make him, if not a more kingly and dignified figure, yet a more living and exuberant personality—his boundless energy, his rude enjoyment of naive pleasures, his blunt, and even coarse, humour. On the other hand, it should not be forgotten that Charlemagne's character has, as we have already had occasion to notice, a curious mediaeval complexity. At times he appears the most simple of kings—a plain and passionate Frank. Yet at other times we detect in him not only a mind working in politics in a fashion extraordinarily tortuous, but also a spiritual disposition, not perhaps of great profundity, but full of strange contrasts. His enthusiasm for religion, and for letters as the vassal of religion, was wholly genuine ; and it is likely that his intimates in the Palace School saw him oftener than we suppose in those deeper moods of kingship which make the ancient Roman title of 'August' an appellation not merely courtly.

III

OTHER AUTHORITIES FOR THE LIFE OF CHARLEMAGNE

BESIDES the *Vita Karoli* of Einhard, our principal authorities for the life of Charlemagne, and the general history of his reign, are the following :—

(1) The *Lorsch Annals* (*Annales Laurissenses*) covering the period from 741–829 This record begins to be a contemporary annual only from the year 788. Down to 796 the author would appear, from internal evidence, to be some official of the Carolingian court. He writes as a partisan, with an obvious hostility towards the Bavarian duchy. The record from 797 to 813 is in a style not unlike that of Einhard ; and Einhard has been conjectured to be the author of this portion. The record

OTHER AUTHORITIES

for the period 813–829 is cited as a work of Einhard by a ninth-century writer; but there are grave difficulties in the way of accepting this ascription.

(2) The *Annals of Einhard*, covering the period 796–829. These are merely an amplification and continuation of the *Lorsch Annals*. The ascription of them to Einhard has no better authority than the caprice of Pertz. The author admits into his narrative incidents which the *Lorsch Annals* found it convenient to omit (e. g. the disaster of Roncesvalles, of which the *Lorsch Annals* say not a word).

(There are two other collections of *Lorsch Annals*, which possess but little authority: (*a*) the *Annales Laurissenses Minores*, 680–718, and (*b*) the *Annales Laureshamenses*, 797–806. Mainly founded on (*b*) is the *Chronicon Moissiacense*.)

(3) The *Moselle Annals* (*Annales Mosellani*), 703–97.

(Mainly founded on these are the Wolfenbuettel, Alemannian, Petau and S. Amand Annals.)

(4) The Life of Charlemagne by the 'Monk of St. Gall'—a largely mythical record, composed in 883, for the pleasure of Charles the Fat.

(5) The Capitularies of Charlemagne.

(6) The *Codex Carolinus*, containing the correspondence of the Frankish kings with the Popes.

(7) *Epistulae Aevi Karolini* (ed. Duemmler).

The literature included under (1)–(3) is collected in the first volume of Pertz's *Monumenta Germaniae Historica* (with others of the minor Chronicles). The Capitularies (5) may be seen in vol. iii of the same collection. (4) and (6) are both consulted most conveniently in the fourth volume of Jaffé's *Bibliotheca Rerum Germanicarum*.

(8) *Liber Pontificalis* (ed. Duchesne): the Lives of Stephen III, Adrian, and Leo III,

IV

GERMAN CULTURE IN THE EARLY MIDDLE AGES

EINHARD speaks of himself, in the Preface to the *Vita Karoli*, as 'homo barbarus et in Romana locutione perparum exercitatus'. Yet no other writer of the Middle Ages has come so near to reproducing the purity and perspicuity of the old *Romana locutio*. When we compare him with the best of his contemporaries—for example, with Alcuin—we feel at once that we are comparing a genuine artist with mere fumblers and botchers. Alcuin was, no doubt, a greater force in that movement of literary and educational reform which we call the Carolingian Renaissance. But if Alcuin was the prime cause—and this is not altogether so certain as we commonly suppose—Einhard is the chief product, of this movement. It is worth asking ourselves whence this movement came, and what are the characteristics of it in that area especially in which Einhard lived and where Charlemagne himself was most truly at home—for in his virtues, as well as in his crying faults, Charlemagne is, after all, essentially German.

The situation of Germany, in respect to the fortunes within its borders of Latin culture, is widely different from that of the other Roman provinces of the continent : it approximates somewhat closely to that of England. Parts of Germany early submitted themselves to Roman influences. Such towns as Mainz, Treves, Salzburg, Ratisbon received a definitely Roman culture. But these influences were not sufficiently strongly established to stand against the barbarian irruptions. They perished

—exactly as the partial Roman culture of England perished in the conflict with Angle, Saxon and Jute. They were restored in the seventh and eighth centuries by the same agencies as, in the sixth century, restored them in England—the missionary movement of Christianity. But the restoration of this culture came to Germany by an oblique path, and not, as to England, direct from Rome. It came to Germany with the books and preaching of the English and Irish missionaries.

The situation of Germany presents, therefore, a strongly marked contrast with that of other continental countries. In Italy, of course, there is an unbroken Latin literary tradition—save in that narrow area of the south which continued to maintain its Greek speech and sympathies all through the middle ages (and in parts of which the Greek language is still in use to-day). Gaul in the third and fourth centuries created a literature superior in quality to that of Rome itself, and possessing, in style and dialect, a marked national character. Spain, from the end of the first century onward, had a genuinely individual culture, and absorbed, as time went on, valuable influences from the great rhetorical schools of Africa—in part transmitting these influences to France. In no century of their history did either Italy, France or Spain cease to produce Latin literature. In all three regions successive barbarian invaders encountered a tradition of speech and writing which they were powerless—had they wished it—to break down. There were reasons why they should not wish to overthrow it; and these deserve consideration here, since they explain the transition from what we call 'classical' to mediaeval Latin, and, incidentally, some of the differences between the mediaeval Latin of Germany and that of other parts of the Empire.

The Latin language, as the universal speech of the Western world, survived the fall of the Western Empire for two reasons :

(1) It was the language not merely of the Empire, but of the Church ;

(2) It was the language both of the civil and of the canon law.

It enshrined, in other words, both the secret of orthodoxy (the Visigoths, when they left their Arianism, abandoned the version of the Scriptures which Ulfilas had made for them) and the secret of organizing conquest. To penetrate these two secrets, it was necessary to pass through the old Roman system of education, in whatever respects modified. The old curriculum of the schools, with their 'standard authors' (who were the same as ours), could not be allowed wholly to perish.

These facts serve to explain at once the general character of what we call the mediaeval Latin. The basis of it is the language of the 'standard authors', above all Cicero and Vergil. This language is modified, firstly, by the language of the Latin translations of the Bible (and hence that strong tincture of both Eastern and Greek idiom, which is the most distinguishing characteristic of mediaeval latinity) ; and, secondly, by the language of law. This latter influence is illustrated in passing in a good many of our Notes to the *Vita Karoli* : but an example which will occur to any one will be the fondness of the mediaeval writers for the expression 'the aforementioned', *praedictus, supradictus, praefatus, memoratus*, &c.—used in contexts purely literary, where no precision or formality is aimed at. The last great influence in the development of mediaeval Latin is— human nature. Human nature demands instruments of expression which are flexible, which are adjusted to the needs of everyday life, and which can be employed by the simple as well as by the highly trained; hence a considerably increased vocabulary, and modifications of grammar and syntax. All these elements go to form what Isidore calls the *lingua mixta*, ' quae post imperium latius promotum simul cum moribus et hominibus in Romanam civitatem inrupit ' (*Etym*. ix. 1. 7).

This *lingua mixta* was the universal medium of Latin culture in the age of Einhard. But here we recur to a distinction which we began by making. In Italy, France, and Spain, this *lingua mixta* was, from the sixth to the ninth century, an integral part of the national life. It was not so in Germany—just as it was not so in England. And here we have what may be called *the explanation of Einhard*. His Latin owes the greater purity of diction, by which it is distinguished from other mediaeval Latin, precisely to the fact that it is necessarily more artificial, that it is drawn with labour from the source and not fetched from any common conduit of literary tradition. It is the Latin of the fifteenth-century Renaissance, and the likeness proceeds from a similarity in the conditions of its origin. Einhard's German Latin is the Latin of a place and time which has never acquired, the Renaissance Latin that of a place and time which has lost, the Roman tradition. We must also allow liberally Einhard's individual talent. The other German Latinists, in comparison, merely stammer Latin.

A useful criterion of culture, over and beyond language, is handwriting. Here is something in which Charlemagne deeply interested himself (see chap. xxv, with notes). Throughout the early Middle Ages, there were two hand-writings in use in the West: the handwriting of the Church (the so-called uncial and half-uncial—developments of capital[1] writing), and the handwriting of the world—the cursive script used for the purposes of business and of law. It was the second of these two hands that the barbarian peoples set themselves to acquire ; and they appear to have taken it with them to the monasteries. There they applied it to the purposes both of religion and of literature. Hence what are called the three great national hands : the Lombardic, or Beneventan, in southern Italy, the Visigothic in Spain, and in France the Merovingian. Of German writing, prior to the Carolingian reform, we have almost no examples—until very recently it was not known that any kind of German national hand had evolved itself. Here again, therefore, we have the same want of tradition as we found in the German use of the Latin language. The object of the Carolingian reform was (1) to remodel the old Merovingian handwriting, which was, of all the national hands, the least legible ; and (2) to create a handwriting for the German monasteries. This reform was carried out mainly with the assistance of English and Irish scholars, who were to be found in plenty not only in the Palace School and in the German monasteries, but also in some of the literary centres of France. These scholars ultimately remodelled the handwriting of the whole of Europe, modifying it on the pattern of the hand out of which their own had originally developed—the old half-uncial writing of the Church.

The impulse towards this reform—which involved a complete reform of education—undoubtedly came from Rome. Its motive is an interest, not in literature as such, but in religion. Better copies of Church books, a better educated clergy—that was what both Charle-

[1] Capital writing survived into the sixth century, but only as a hand for *éditions de luxe* of the great classics.

magne and Alcuin were primarily interested in. Yet it is possible to exaggerate the purely ecclesiastical nature of this great movement. It covers a wide area, and among the assistants of Charlemagne must have been many who, like Einhard, had entered by an inner line into the spirit of the ancient secular literature—or of parts of it. Moreover, the nature of any literary interest is such that it is never satisfied with prescribed bounds. The enthusiasm for antiquity inevitably carries those who feel it further than they design to go. Only so can we explain the preservation, in copies made in the Carolingian period, of so many ancient Latin writers who were of no service to religion, and could not be reckoned among the few 'standard authors' who were the basis of school-teaching.

One great effect of the educational reforms of Charlemagne, which seems sometimes to be lost sight of, is the linking up of the great monasteries of Europe. We enter upon a great era of intercommunication between both near and distant literary centres. The letters of the time sufficiently illustrate this—in particular the correspondence of Servatus Lupus. Germany reaped the full benefit of this intercourse with other centres of learning, importing not only scholars and books, but a tradition; until in the tenth century the German monasteries (Mainz, Fulda, Treves, Cologne, Bamberg, Hersfeld, Lorsch, Würzburg, Reichenau, St. Gall) are among the principal copying schools of Europe.

Einhard mentions casually in chap. xxix a subject more interesting to posterity than he, perhaps, with his very Latin outlook, was likely to suppose—the native German literature. He tells us that Charlemagne caused to be copied, and that he learned by heart, 'barbara et antiquissima carmina, quibus veterum regum actus et bella canebantur'; and that he even set about preparing a grammar of the German language. That there existed in Charlemagne's time a considerable body of Frankish heroic poetry is attested by the fact that the later German saga has its theme in the warfares and migrations of the fifth century, and, therefore, grew from this earlier poetry. There existed also in the Carolingian period a certain amount of German prose literature, which Einhard does not here mention. It consisted mainly of religious writings (sermons, translations), which were a weak vernacular imitation of Latin monastic work of the time. On this it is likely that Charlemagne, in his zeal for the Roman Church, looked with no particular favour. His son and successor, Louis the Pious, looked with great *disfavour* on the ' barbara carmina ', which his father tolerated : ' nec legere, nec audire, nec docere voluit ', says Thegan (chap. xix). It is possibly owing to this prejudice of Louis that these lays have been lost to us. Charlemagne's interest in them says nothing, of course, for their merits. He may very well have been guided here not only by his Frankish temperament, but also by Alcuin. Bede, who was the teacher of Alcuin's teacher Egbert, and whose authority lived long in York, where Alcuin was educated, took the same liberal view of the vernacular literature of his own country.[1]

We append here the Capitulary of Charlemagne *De Litteris Colendis*, sometimes called the *Letter to Baugulfus*, but in reality an Encyclical. As the official expression of the educational ideal of the age, it is a document of first-rate interest and importance, involving the whole fate of European letters. It is given in Pertz, *Monumenta Germaniae Historica*, iii, pp. 52-3, and in Jaffé, *Bibliotheca*

---

[1] See Bede, *Eccl. Hist.* iv. 24, Plummer I, lxxiv, clxi.

Rerum Germanicarum, iv, pp. 343-4 ; but as neither book is easily accessible to the average student, it has been thought worth while to print the whole document [1] here :—

'Karolus gratia Dei Rex Francorum et Langobardorum ac Patricius Romanorum Baugulfo Abbati et omni congregationi, tibi etiam commissis fidelibus oratoribus nostris, in Omnipotentis Dei nomine amabilem direximus salutem.

' Notum igitur sit Deo placitae devotioni vestrae, quia nos una cum fidelibus nostris consideravimus utile esse ut episcopia et monasteria, nobis Christo propitio commissa, praeter regularis vitae ordinem atque sanctae Religionis conversationem etiam in litterarum meditationibus eos qui, donante Domino, discere possunt, secundum unius cuiusque capacitatem discendi studium debeant impendere : qualiter, sicut regularis norma honestatem morum, ita quoque docendi et discendi instantia ordinet et ornet seriem verborum : ut qui Deo placere appetunt recte vivendo, ei etiam placere non neglegant recte loquendo. Scriptum est enim, *Aut ex verbis tuis iustificaberis aut ex verbis tuis condemnaberis.* Quamvis enim melius sit bene facere quam nosse, prius tamen est nosse quam facere. Debet ergo quisque discere quod optat implere, ut tanto uberius quid agere debeat intellegat anima quanto in Omnipotentis Dei laudibus sine mendaciorum offendiculis cucurrerit lingua. Nam cum omnibus hominibus vitanda sint mendacia, quanto magis illi secundum possibilitatem declinare debent qui ad hoc solummodo probantur electi, ut servire specialiter debeant veritati.

' Nam cum nobis in his annis a nonnullis monasteriis

[1] With it may be read the Encyclical *De Emendatione Librorum*, Pertz, III, 44 sq.

saepius scripta dirigerentur, in quibus quid pro nobis fratres ibidem commorantes in sacris et piis orationibus significaretur, cognovimus in plurimis praefatis conscriptionibus eorundem et sensus rectos et sermones incultos ; quia, quod pia devotio interius fideliter dictabat, hoc exterius propter neglegentiam discendi inerudita exprimere sine reprehensione non valebat.

'Unde factum est ut timere inciperemus ne forte, sicut minor erat in scribendo prudentia, ita quoque et multo minor esset quam esse debuisset in Sanctarum Scripturarum ad intellegendum sapientia.

'Quamobrem hortamur vos : Litterarum studia non neglegere, verum etiam humillima et Deo placita intentione ad hoc certatim discere, ut facilius et rectius divinarum Scripturarum mysteria valeatis penetrare. Cum enim in sacris paginis schemata tropi et cetera his similia inserta inveniantur, nulli dubium quod ea unus quisque legens tanto citius spiritualiter intellegit quanto prius in litteraturae magisterio plenius instructus fuerit. Tales vero ad hoc opus viri eligantur qui et voluntatem et possibilitatem discendi et desiderium habeant alios instruendi. Et hoc totum ea intentione agatur qua devotione a nobis praecipitur. Optamus enim vos, sicut decet milites, et interius devotos et exterius doctos castosque bene vivendo et scholasticos bene loquendo, ut quicunque vos propter Nomen Domini et sanctae conversationis nobilitatem ad videndum expetierit, sicut de aspectu vestro aedificatur visus, ita quoque de sapientia vestra, quam in legendo seu cantando perceperit, instructus, Omnipotenti Domino gratias agendo gaudens redeat.

'Huius itaque epistulae exemplaria ad omnes suffragantes tuosque coepiscopos et per universa monasteria dirigi non neglegas, si gratiam nostram habere vis. Et nullus monachus foras monasterio iudiciaria teneatur nec per mallos et publica placita pergat.

' Legens valeat.'

The debt of Literature to the Carolingian copying-schools may be best brought home to us by a very simple consideration. If we set aside Catullus, Tibullus, Propertius, and Silius Italicus, together with the Tragedies of Seneca and parts of Statius and Claudian, we owe the preservation of practically the whole of Latin poetry to the scholars of the time of Charlemagne. These same scholars have preserved to us, except for Varro, Tacitus, Apuleius, practically the whole of the prose literature of Rome. Without what they thus preserved to us we should not have had the Renaissance, and we should have had, as a consequence, either no literature of modern Europe or a literature wholly different both in form and substance.

It would be ungrateful here, however, not to remember the contribution to Learning of a part of the Roman world which never came within the empire of Charlemagne—the Lombard Duchy of Benevento. The Beneventans developed a book-hand of their own of great beauty, and for three centuries, little influenced by the Carolingian reform, they copied in this hand the great classical writers of Rome. They have preserved to us some authors whom the Carolingians missed ; and of authors copied by the Carolingians they have sometimes preserved to us a better text. The chief centre of Beneventan culture was the monastery of Monte Cassino —that monastery in which Carloman, the uncle of Charlemagne, found a refuge from the cares of kingship.

V

THE CAROLINGIAN EMPIRE: ITS LIMITS AND ADMINISTRATION

§ 1.—Limits.

EINHARD in chapter xv of the *Vita Karoli* describes the limits of the Carolingian empire as they were in the last years of the Emperor's life after the great wars. Charlemagne, says Einhard, had doubled the territories of his father Pepin. In his empire were included Gaul from the Rhine to the Pyrenees; Spain, from the Pyrenees to the river Ebro; Germany from the Rhine to the Elbe, from the North Sea to the Alps; all Italy, excepting Calabria; on the eastern shores of the Adriatic, Istria, Liburnia, and Dalmatia, except the maritime cities. Besides these there were, as tributaries, all the lands of the Slavs between the Elbe and the Vistula, and also Pannonia and Dacia.[1] Thus the western limit of the Empire was the Ebro, the eastern limits, the Vistula and Theiss.[2]

[1] See notes to chap. xv. Ancient Dacia lay to the *East* of the River Theiss, but it is unlikely that Charlemagne had any real authority there.

[2] Theodulf, Bishop of Orleans, in his *Versus contra iudices* (*Poetae Latini Medii Aevi*, ed. Duemmler, i. 496), states the rivers of Charlemagne's dominions thus, without mentioning the Ebro:—

    Cui parent Walis, Rodanus, Mosa, Renus et Henus,
      Sequana, Wisurgis, Wardo, Garonna, Padus,
    Rura, Mosella, Liger, Volturnus, Matrona, Ledus,
      Hister, Atax, Gabarus, Olitis, Albis, Arar.

[... Waal, Rhone, Meuse, Rhine, Inn, Seine, Weser, Gard (tributary of Rhone), Garonne, Po, Roer, Moselle, Loire, Volturno (north of Naples), Marne, Lez (near Montpellier), Danube, Aude (in Languedoc), Gave (in Bearn), Lot, Elbe, Saône.]

ITS LIMITS AND ADMINISTRATION xliii

In this impressive picture of Einhard some exceptions must be noticed. Spain between the Ebro and the Pyrenees was not conquered by Charlemagne. The expedition of 778 was a strong military demonstration, but it accomplished no permanent subjection of the country. Only so much of Spain as lay between the Pyrenees and a line drawn from Pampeluna to Barcelona was actually administered by Charlemagne's officials. In Gaul itself, the isolated, rocky country of Brittany, and the land of the impetuous Gascons,[1] were left to their native dukes. In Italy, the Eastern (Byzantine) Emperors held, in addition to Naples, Venice, which Charlemagne renounced in 812. The Duchy of Benevento, which hovered between allegiance to the Eastern and Western Emperors, was only tributary (since 812), and in the States of the Church (the Exarchate of Ravenna, the Pentapolis, the Patrimony of St. Peter) Pope Leo III enjoyed practically complete independence from Charlemagne.

But even with these qualifications, the Empire of Charlemagne remains perhaps the most impressive fact in European history. Under his vigorous hand, Europe came nearer than ever before or since to the ideal of Christian unity. In spite of his private faults and his almost continual wars, Charlemagne built up a huge state, governed explicitly through principles of morality, peace, Christianity. The unity of the Empire lay in himself, in the acknowledgment of his power, and of these principles on which he based his power.

But beneath this imperial unity there was some diversity: three different kinds of dominion existed within the limits of the Carolingian empire. In the first place there were the countries ruled directly by Charle-

[1] Einhard, chap. v, *L'Art de vérifier les dates*, ii. 254.

magne himself or by his vice-gerents, who were his sons, the kings Pepin, Louis, Charles. These countries were Gaul, Germany, Italy (with the exceptions already noted). In 781 Charlemagne made his youngest son Louis King of Aquitaine, and Pepin his second son King of Italy. In 806 at Thionville, the Emperor made another division, making Charles, his eldest son, King of Gaul (except Aquitaine) and of most of Germany; the kingdoms of Aquitaine and Italy remained to Louis and Pepin respectively, with certain important additions. But these divisions, this establishment of kings under the Emperor, made no difference to the imperial unity, to the Carolingian administration. The kings were really vice-gerents: the system of government, by *Counts* and *Missi*, was the same as before; the kingdoms remained subject to legislation, when Charlemagne, in a general Assembly, issued a *Capitulary* which directly applied to all the Empire. The kings also could, with the assent of their own Assemblies, issue *Capitularies* applying to their own kingdoms. The elevation of Louis in 813 as colleague and Emperor with Charlemagne, made no difference to the imperial system of government.

The tributaries, the tribes between the Elbe and Vistula, and the peoples about the middle Danube, are not to be considered as strictly within the Empire. The acknowledgment of the dominion of Charlemagne generally lasted only as long as the particular punitive expedition which he sent among these peoples. As regularly paid tributes are not mentioned, it is to be gathered that the presence of Charlemagne's power was not continuously felt. The Emperor does not even seem to have secured more than a nominal acceptance of Christianity among the Slavs and Hungarians. In the war of 797, Tudun, one of the chiefs of the Hungarians, allowed himself to be baptized, but Hungary remained a heathen country for over two hundred years more. The last tributary to be mentioned, Benevento, was more closely connected with the Carolingian Empire, for in 812 its Duke Grimoaldo paid a sum of 25,000 golden *solidi*.

The States of the Church were in a totally different position from the Empire proper and from the tributaries. The Pope was not merely the spiritual head of Christendom, he had also the temporal power over the central part of Italy. Rome and the surrounding province, making up together the ' Patrimony of St. Peter ', had enjoyed a certain amount of independence since the time of Pope Gregory the Great. In addition to these dominions the Popes claimed the town and district of Ravenna, which had been ruled by a Byzantine exarch or governor till 751, when it was taken by the Lombards. In 754, Pope Stephen II had called upon Pepin the Short, father of Charlemagne, to come and help him against the Lombards. This was the beginning of Frankish power in Italy. The Pope at St. Denis anointed Pepin as King of the Franks, and made him ' Patrician ' of the Roman Republic. In return for these privileges Pepin could not do less than guarantee the immunity and independence of the States of the Church, which the Papacy from that time claimed to include Rome and the Exarchate of Ravenna and the Pentapolis (Ancona, Pesaro, Fano, Sinigaglia, Umana). The exact terms of Pepin's ' donation ' of 754 are unknown. In 774, Charlemagne came to Italy under somewhat similar circumstances to those of his father, and renewed with Pope Hadrian I the donation of Pepin. Charlemagne seems also to have promised certain great additions, including Spoleto and Benevento.[1] In effect the Papacy had by the year 787 received an addition of several Tuscan cities : Soana, Toscanella, Viterbo, Bagnorea. Thus the Papacy held a large part of Italy, from the mouth of the Adige on the north-east, to the March of Ancona on the east, and on the west from the River Cecina to Terracina. Within these 'States' the Pope was sovereign, and Charlemagne, who owed all his legal position in Italy to the Papacy, could not help respecting the claim. He himself was Patrician of the Roman Republic, and as such his duty was to protect it. The States of the Church were therefore not properly part of the Carolingian Empire, and it is to be noticed that Charlemagne never claimed to have his capital in Rome. Indeed so far was the Papacy from admitting the States of the Church to be within the Empire, that Hadrian I and succeeding Popes always maintained that in strict law the Empire was within the States of the Church. A 'donation' of the Emperor Constantine was produced, which purported to have granted to Pope Sylvester I all Italy and all the West. This donation was undoubtedly a forgery of somebody, but Hadrian received it as genuine, and from that time the Popes claimed to be superior to the Emperors. It is clear therefore that the 'States of the Church', in the narrower sense of the term, were at least not an integral part of the Carolingian Empire.

[1] The boundaries of the Donation of Charlemagne as given in the *Vita Hadriani* (*Liber Pontificalis*, ed. Duchesne, i. 498) are very large. They are: 'a Lunis cum insula Corsica, deinde in Suriano, deinde in monte Bardone, id est in Verceto, deinde in Parma, deinde in Regio; et exinde in Mantua atque Monte Silicis, simulque et universum exarchatum Ravennantium, sicut antiquitus erat, atque provincias Venetiarum et Istria; necnon et cunctum ducatum Spolitinum seu Beneventanum.'

Within the limits of the Empire as thus described, from Barcelona to the Elbe, there was no administrative centre : the Empire had no capital. The central government consisted of the household, the domestic officials of Charlemagne : there was no distinction between the Palace staff and the Administration. Wherever Charlemagne happened to be living, the Administration went with him. He had several favourite places of abode, among which Rome cannot be numbered, nor Paris, which he perhaps never saw. In France he often resided at Compiègne, Attigny, Quierzy; in Germany, at Thionville, Worms, Schlestadt, Frankfort-on-Main, Aix-la-Chapelle ; also at Nimeguen, Mainz, Worms, Ratisbon. But Aix was his favourite residence ; there were his chief palace, his own chapel, his baths. There he held most of the legislative assemblies ; there was his treasury, and there ultimately he found his tomb. The Rhineland was the geographical and the educational centre of Charlemagne's Empire ; and Aix was, in a greater degree than any other place, the administrative capital.

§ 2.—ADMINISTRATION.

The constitution of any country is usually divided into legislative, administrative, and judicial. In the Carolingian Empire the legislative machinery had a separate existence, but the administrative and judicial functions, as frequently happens even now, were in the same hands.

The Emperor was the head of the whole imperial system, not merely in law, but in fact. How much the Empire depended upon the mighty personality of Charlemagne is proved by the decline which took place after his death. The will of the Emperor was absolute ;

his 'ban' or command could not be denied or questioned: 'that no one in any way presume to mar any ban or precept of the lord emperor, nor to discuss nor hinder nor diminish his work, and that no one in any respect act contrary to his will or precepts.'[1] Such was the theory of the absolute power of the Emperor: in practice his power was limited, not so much in administrative matters, but in legislation. A large number of the capitularies were passed in an Assembly or convention of the great lay and ecclesiastical personages of the Empire, and in the presence of at least some of the lower classes. But some capitularies have no preamble, stating the consent of the general assembly, and it is to be presumed that they issued directly from the Emperor and his standing council, and were taken by the *missi* into the provinces, and there put in force without question.

The Emperor was certainly supreme in administration and justice. He could make and unmake any official, he could hear any cases of law, either by way of original jurisdiction or by appeal. As a rule, he limited his judicial functions to hearing appeals, and even then only when all the lower sources of justice had been tried, sometimes as often as three times. The Emperor himself could not frequently hear cases in person: but the *missi* who went on circuit every year, supervising justice and administration, owed all their powers to the personal and indisputable authority of the Emperor. As a last resort, when the local Counts failed to settle cases, and the *Missi* proved inadequate, disputes might be called to the royal

---

[1] 'Ut nullum bannum vel preceptum domni imperatori nullus omnino in nullo marrire praesumat, neque opus eius tricare vel impedire, vel minuere, vel in alia contrarius fierit voluntati vel preceptis eius.' *Capitulare Aquisgranense*, anno 802, cap. 8, in *M G. H*. III. i. 92, Pertz.

ITS LIMITS AND ADMINISTRATION xlix

palace. If the Emperor did not hear them in person, the duty was discharged by the Count of the Palace.

Absolute in theory, and wielding enormous powers in practice, the Emperor nevertheless could not dispense with a standing council of men, on whom he could rely. This council, like the Curia Regis of the Angevin Kings of England, consisted of the chief officials and ecclesiastics who by the nature of their functions would be most constantly with the sovereign, and would know most about the affairs of the State. Their number was not precisely fixed, but three were always together with Charlemagne, and without their advice he seems to have done nothing.

In ecclesiastical affairs the Emperor was no less powerful than in secular matters. In all the lands won from the pagan, where he himself established bishoprics and abbeys, the appointments to high benefices remained in his own hands. In the other parts of his dominions, where Christianity was of old standing, the election of bishops by the chapter with the assent of the local *populus* was maintained, subject to the license of the Emperor, conveyed in a royal letter. Matters of legislation which affected the Church were dealt with in the regular assemblies held by Charlemagne at Aix and elsewhere ; and even when special ecclesiastical councils met to consider questions of doctrine, Charlemagne in important instances presided and took the chief part in the decision. Such instances are the Synod of Frankfort in 794, which condemned the heresy of 'Adoptianism', and the Synod of Aix in 809, which settled that *Filioque* should be inserted in the Creed after *qui ex Patre procedit*. Thus in his position with regard to the lay official class, and to the ecclesiastical hierarchy and the Church, Charlemagne held and even extended the lofty powers

d

which had come down with the Merovingian tradition of kingship.

The great Assemblies of the Carolingian Empire met frequently, generally in May. In theory these were probably the old Germanic assemblies of all the freemen. In Charlemagne's time the people were supposed to be present. In reality, the Assembly consisted of bishops, abbots, and counts, with their followers. The people were, therefore, only represented by these followers, or by the inhabitants of the town in which the Assembly happened to be held. The great men deliberated inside the palace; the ' people ' remained outside, and received the results of the deliberations which were carried on within. The Emperor took part in the meetings inside the palace, and also moved about and mixed with the people outside. Sometimes, when a Capitulary was to be passed affecting a particular part of the Empire, members of all classes of freemen were summoned to attend. The *Capitulare Saxonicum* (October 28, 797) states in its preamble that it was drawn up and agreed to in an assembly in the palace at Aix of bishops, abbots, and counts, and a congregation of Saxons from various regions, both Westphalians, Angrarians, and Ostphalians.[1]

Any sort of subject was within the competence of the great Assembly. A large number of Capitularies deal with ecclesiastical affairs, others with the way in which *missi* should behave in their itineraries, and in which counts should behave in their localities; others make additions or corrections to the particular code of laws

[1] '. . . convenientibus in unum Aquis palatio in eius obsequio venerabilibus episcopis et abbatibus, seu inlustris viris comitibus, V. Kal. Nov., simulque congregatis Saxonibus de diversis pagis, tam de Westfalahis et Angrariis, quam et de Oostfalahis, omnes unianimiter consenserunt et aptificaverunt . . .', *M. G. H.* III. i. 75, Pertz.

ITS LIMITS AND ADMINISTRATION

current in some of the integral countries of the empire; others deal with coinage or fiscal matters. The tone of all the Capitularies is deeply moral: precepts concerning good conduct, integrity of purpose, duty, compassion towards widows, orphans, the poor, appear on nearly every page. The whole work of the Assemblies makes a slender enough volume compared with modern statute books, but it is a noble monument of the ideals of the age. Everything is dealt with in a broad ample fashion: questions of detail and the application of the principles of the Capitularies are left to the discretion of those who have to carry them out.

The great Assembly—the *generalis* or *synodalis conventus*—which met nearly every year, in summer, was often succeeded in autumn by a smaller Assembly, which met to prepare the business for the following summer's meeting. It dealt also with matters of urgency, such as war. In character it was a restricted form of the *generalis conventus*: none of the *populus* was present, and only the greatest of the ecclesiastics and counts.

Such was the legislative machinery of Charlemagne's Empire. The administrative machinery was more highly organized, and is indeed the most striking feature of the imperial system. The official class was divided into central and local, with the *missi dominici* as a link between the two. The central officials were simply the palace staff of the Emperor; in name and in origin they were merely domestic. The chief is no longer the Mayor of the Palace as in Merovingian times; he is now called the Count of the Palace (*comes palatii*), in other respects the *ministeriales palatini* are little different from the palace hierarchy of the Merovingian period. Their functions were necessarily both public and private, as no distinction was made between the public and private revenues of the Emperor, between himself as a man and as a magistrate. In his palace were his rooms for sleeping and eating; also the treasury, the archives, the courts of justice, the council-chamber, the hall for the *generalis conventus*. The Emperor's personal habits were simple: the purely domestic work of his officials could be performed by a few deputies. The real work of the chamberlains, the butlers, the seneschals, and the chaplains was to carry on the Carolingian administration, to deal with war, revenue, justice; to each of the great functionaries an office was given: in one the count gave out justice, in another the chancellor and his notaries drew up royal letters, elsewhere the archchaplain preserved the duplicates, and stored the archives of the monarch.

The residence of the Emperor, sometimes in one place, sometimes in another, but most frequently at Aix, was thus the centre of administration: its officials were numerous, its business large. It was a real bureaucracy, with the skill and experience which such a permanent body acquires: open also to the evils, corruption, and profligacy, which the possession of power, especially when combined, as in this instance, with the atmosphere of an immoral court, is apt to produce. But Charlemagne had a keen eye for corruption both among the palace ministers and the local counts. The Capitulary *de disciplina palatii* was an honest and vigorous attempt to cope with the evil. Each *ministerialis palatinus* was made responsible for himself and all his assistants and men: he was to make careful inquisition for all evil-livers, all quarrelers, all venal persons; and once a week, on Sunday, he had to make a report to the Emperor on the result of his investigations. The penalties for ill

ITS LIMITS AND ADMINISTRATION

discipline were severe, and were to be administered without exceptions of persons or sex.[1]

The local administration was also highly organized. Although the old names of provinces continue, Septimania, Neustria, Alemannia, and others, these provinces had, under Charlemagne, no separate legal existence; there were no great Dukes; all provinces were divided into counties, in much the same way as the well-known provinces of France are now divided into departments. The only divisions of the Empire which had a separate administrative existence were the 'kingdoms' of Aquitaine and Lombardy, under Louis and Pepin, and the Marches, the exposed frontier districts—the Marches of Brittany, Spain, Friuli, Bavaria—each of which was under a *praefectus*, who was responsible for its defence. The existence of the kingdoms made no difference to the local administration: both Aquitaine and Lombardy were divided into counties, and regularly visited by *missi*.

The Empire was divided into about 300 counties; the exact number cannot be ascertained, but they seem to have been fairly equally divided, in proportion to the size of the country, between France, Germany, and Italy. The county varied greatly in size: sometimes it was confined to one small town and district, sometimes it included a whole region, like Auvergne. The count was like the mediaeval English sheriff; he heard cases of justice; he collected the fiscal dues of the Emperor; he called out the freemen to attend the host when the Emperor was at war. Closely associated with him was the bishop, who was charged with supporting the authority of the count in all possible ways, and with applying the instructions of the Emperor to priests, just

[1] *M. G. H.* III. i. 158–9, Pertz.

as the count applied them to laymen. The affairs of Church and State were often mingled in everyday life. The count and bishop were colleagues, like the Emperor and Pope. But their relations were not strictly defined, and misunderstandings and even quarrels were by no means unknown.

The *missi dominici* connected the central authorities and the local, the Palace and the County. These *missi* were great officials sent from the Emperor to inspect the method of local administration, to hear important cases of justice, to take the oaths of allegiance to the Emperor. Just as the whole Empire was divided into fixed counties, so it was also divided into permanent *missatica,* one *missaticum* including, on the average, seven to ten counties.[1] The *missi* were without particular interests in the localities, and they made their journeys in pairs, a palace count and a bishop together, the temporal and the spiritual being a complement and also a check to each other.

But sometimes two ecclesiastics were sent together, instead of one layman and one clergyman. The poem of Theodulf, Bishop of Orleans, *Versus contra iudices,*[2] as an instance of the difficulties and temptations which beset judges, describes a journey of himself as *missus,* along with Laidradus who was a Bavarian and a clerk, and who subsequently became Archbishop of Lyons. The two *missi* started from Lyons, and going down the Rhone, first stopped at Vienne. From there they proceeded to Valence, then to all the places of any size in the valley of the Rhone or in Septimania: Orange,

[1] Two Missatica will be found in the *Capitula Missis Dominicis Data,* in *M. G. H.,* Pertz, III. i. 96. They are *Missaticum Parisiense et Rodomense* and *Missaticum Senonense.*

[2] Duemmler, *Poetae Latini Medii Aevi,* i. 493 ff.

Avignon, Nîmes, Béziers, Narbonne, Carcassonne. From Carcassonne the *missi* went back to Arles. Marseilles, Aix(-les-Bains), and Cavaillon completed the itinerary. At every stopping-place the *missi* held a court, and listened to the suits of clergy and people, and inquired into the administration of the law. From all sides bribes were frankly offered to the *missi*; one man would promise gems, if he should be adjudged the land of his neighbour; another would offer Saracen gold coins, or Italian silver coins, in return for a verdict giving him estates, lands, houses. Others, more delicate, would secretly take the *minister*, the attendant official of one of the *missi*, aside, and would describe in glowing detail some precious piece of plate, and would let it be known that he would give it to his (the petitioner's) 'lord' (i.e. the *missus*), if the verdict in the law-suit was favourable. Corruption, the offering of bribes, was found in every class of people, and the acceptance of the bribes among every sort of judge.[1] But Theodulf was inaccessible to bribes, and gave out justice with an even hand. Yet in order that he might not make himself remarkable, nor hurt the feelings of those suitors who offered presents out of kindness, he accepted some small but pleasing gifts for the table: ripe fruits, eggs, wine, loaves of bread, oats, tender chickens and small birds, whose bodies are small but good for food. This action he commends: stern virtue is proper when tempered with discretion.[2] It is clear that judicial and administrative corruption

---

[1] 'O scelerata lues, partes diffusa per omnes,
    O scelus, o furor, o res truculenta nimis.
  Quae sibi captivum totum male vindicat orbem
    Nec deest, qui det, nec qui male capta ferat.'—ll. 255–8.

[2] 'O felix omnis virtus, discretio si quam
    Virtutum nutrix temperat, ornat, alit.'—ll. 289, 290.

was an evil deeply rooted in the Carolingian Empire: but it is also clear that the existence of the evil was recognized, and that efforts were always being made to deal with it.

The principle at the base of the Carolingian administration was to throw the responsibility as much as possible on the local authorities. The real work of government was discharged by the local counts; the central government, the Palace, confined itself almost entirely to the business of supervision. For this reason, the financial system of the Empire was very simple: each county found the funds for its own administration. Therefore the amount of money which the central government had to raise for itself, amounted to comparatively little. The business of the Palace was to organize: the business of the county was to execute and to pay its own expenses. The only expenses incurred by the central government were the expenses of the Palace. Even wars which affected the whole Empire were paid for by the localities. Each count and bishop had to find men from their own district; and the district had to provide for almost all the expenses of the troops which it sent.

Since, therefore, almost the only expenses of the central government were the upkeep of the Palace staff, there was no distinction between the public and private income of the Emperor. His revenues were drawn from three chief sources: firstly, his own domain, which was very large, and consisted of estates situated in various parts of the Empire; secondly, the tribute paid by conquered peoples, the Slavonic tribes, the Beneventans; thirdly, booty. The Empire was almost continually at war on one frontier or another, and the booty was partly taken into the imperial treasury at Aix, partly distributed among the soldiers, and partly given to the

Church. In addition to the above-mentioned sources of income, there were the annual gifts which the great men of the Empire brought to the sovereign when they came to the Assembly each year; and also the fees of the palace court, when law-suits were brought to the Emperor for settlement. But the greatest source of revenue by far was probably the produce of the imperial domain—the Emperor's farms, woods, and forests. These were very carefully administered, as may be seen from the long and interesting Capitulary on the Imperial *Vills* issued in 812.[1]

The expenses which the local counties had to meet were fairly numerous. Food and lodging had to be found for the Emperor and his staff, whenever he visited a town and district. Similarly, the entertainment of the *missi* had to be provided for. Secondly, forced labour, *la corvée*, was a severe tax upon each district: all public works, roads, bridges (such as the great bridge at Mainz which Charlemagne built) or the canal which he left partially dug out between the Rhine and Danube, were performed by forced labour which the counts requisitioned. Finally, the military *stipendia* which the localities had to provide must have been very great: that part of the Empire which would benefit most from the war provided the most soldiers: distant provinces had to send proportionately less men, on account of the long way they had to travel. On their way, the troops could claim water, wood, and forage from the district through which they passed; but they had to bring their own food, or the money to provide it, for three months. Each man provided his own arms, of a kind suited to his means.

The obligation of military service was intended to

[1] *Capitulare de Villis Imperialibus*, *M.G.H.*, Pertz, III. i. 181–7.

fall only upon 'free men', that is to say, on all who had no lord above them save the Emperor. For each expedition, a certain number of landowners were ordered from each province: a substantial proprietor came in person; smaller proprietors were joined together to provide a man. Landless men who were free had to serve if they possessed movable property. They had to attend the host in person if they were rich; or by joining each with five others to provide one man, if each possessed only five *solidi*.[1]

Such in outline was the administrative system of Charlemagne. The resemblance between it and the institutions of the Anglo-Saxons, the Normans, and the Plantagenets, has attracted many inquirers: the count was like the Norman sheriff, the *missus* did precisely the work of an itinerant baron of the Angevin Exchequer or Curia. The *scabini* or freemen who had to attend the count's court, to assist him with their counsel, are scarcely to be distinguished from a jury; the *comites* who lived near the Emperor's palace and were bound to serve him anywhere at any time, have affinities to the Saxon thegns and gesiths.

Freedom was at the root of the Carolingian administration. Slaves existed in plenty, but they played no part in justice or administration; there were no 'freedmen' in the Palace. Even the tenant or sworn follower of another man was considered unfree. The tenants and vassals of the Emperor himself were not *liberi*. But the body of landed free proprietors was not sufficient to supply the military needs of the Empire: the large and growing number of men who held land from a great man or from the Emperor had to be called upon. When the 'heriban', the summons to the host, is directed to

[1] *Capitulare Aquense* Anni 807, *M. G. H.*, Pertz, III. i. 149.

these 'beneficed' men, the 'feudal system' begins to appear in Europe.[1]

But it was only a beginning. Government was still free: no one could deal out justice, no one could order the public life of any section of the people, who had not been authorized to do so by the Emperor. Rulers and judges had no hereditary rights, no position of authority, as landowners or tenants. The people were not yet divided firmly into 'those who fought, those who prayed, and those who worked with their hands'. The clergy were a class apart, the slaves tilled their lords' ground, but the bulk of the people were free and no man's vassal. The freeman, rich or poor, was eligible for any office under the Emperor; it was his duty and privilege to fight, but not as any lord's man. If he was poor, and worked with his own hands, he was still a *liber homo*, and in the eye of the law greater than the greatest 'vassal', and the equal of the proudest 'count'.

[1] *Capitulare de exercitu promovendo*, 803. In *M. G. H.*, Pertz, III. i. 119, cap. 5.

MANUSCRIPTS

A	Codex Vindobonensis, Bibl. Pal. 510	saec. ix
B	Codex Montepessulanus, 360	saec. ix–x
b	Codex Vindobonensis, Bibl. Pal. 473	saec. x
C	Codex Parisinus, 10758	saec. ix–x

WALAHFRIDI PROLOGUS

GLORIOSISSIMI imperatoris Karoli vitam et gesta, quae subiecta sunt, Einhardus, vir inter omnes huius temporis palatinos non solum pro scientia, verum et pro universa morum honestate laudis egregiae, descripsisse cognoscitur et purissimae veritatis, utpote qui his paene omnibus interfuerit, testimonio roborasse. Natus enim in orientali Francia, in pago qui dicitur Moingeuui, in Fuldensi coenobio sub pedagogio sancti Bonifacii martiris prima puerilis nutriturae rudimenta suscepit. Indeque potius propter singularitatem capacitatis et intelligentiae, quae iam tum in illo magnum, quod postea claruit, specimen sapientiae promittebat, quam ob nobilitatis, quod in eo munus erat insigne, a Baugulfo abbate monasterii supradicti in palatium Karoli translatus est; quippe qui omnium regum avidissimus erat sapientes diligenter inquirere et, ut cum omni delectatione philosopharentur, excolere; ideoque regni a Deo sibi commissi nebulosam et, ut ita dicam, paene caecam latitudinem totius scientiae nova irradiatione et huic barbariei ante partim incognita luminosam reddidit Deo illustrante atque videntem. Nunc vero relabentibus in contraria studiis lumen sapientiae, quod minus diligitur, rarescit in plurimis. Praedictus itaque homuncio — nam statura despicabilis videbatur — in aula Karoli, amatoris scientiae, tantum gloriae incrementum merito prudentiae et probitatis est assecutus, ut inter omnes regiae maiestatis ministros paene nullus haberetur, cui rex id temporis potentissimus et sapientissimus plura familiaritatis suae secreta committeret. Et re vera non immerito, cum non modo ipsius Karoli temporibus, sed et — quod maioris miraculi est — sub Ludowico imperatore, cum multis et diversis perturbationibus Francorum res publica fluctuaret et in multis decideret, mira quadam et divinitus provisa libratione se ipsum Deo protegente custodierit, ut sublimitatis nomen, quod multis invidiam comparavit et casum, ipsum nec immature deseruerit nec periculis irremediabilibus manciparit. Haec dicimus, ut in dictis eius minus quisque habeat dubitationis, dum non ignoret eum et dilectioni provectoris sui laudem praecipuam et curiositati lectoris veritatem debere perspicuam. Huic opusculo ego Strabo titulos et incisiones, prout visum est congruum, inserui, ut ad singula facilior quaerenti quod placuerit elucescat accessus.

VITA KAROLI IMPERATORIS AB EINHARDO DICTATA

Vitam et conversationem et ex parte non modica res gestas domini et nutritoris mei Karoli, excellentissimi et merito famosissimi regis, postquam scribere animus tulit, quanta potui brevitate conplexus sum, operam inpendens ut de his quae ad meam notitiam pervenire potuerunt nihil omitterem neque prolixitate narrandi nova quaeque fastidientium animos offenderem; si tamen hoc ullo modo vitari potest, ut nova scriptione non offendantur qui vetera et a viris doctissimis atque disertissimis confecta monumenta fastidiunt. Et quamquam plures esse non ambigam, qui otio ac litteris dediti statum aevi praesentis non arbitrentur ita neglegendum, ut omnia penitus quae nunc fiunt velut nulla memoria digna silentio atque oblivioni tradantur, potiusque velint amore diuturnitatis inlecti aliorum praeclara facta qualibuscumque scriptis inserere quam sui nominis famam posteritatis memoriae nihil scribendo subtrahere, tamen ab huiuscemodi scriptione non existimavi temperandum, quando mihi conscius eram nullum ea veracius quam me scribere posse, quibus ipse interfui, quaeque praesens oculata, ut dicunt, fide cognovi et utrum ab alio scriberentur necne liquido scire non potui. Satiusque iudicavi eadem cum aliis velut communiter litteris mandata memoriae posterorum tradere quam regis excellentissimi et omnium sua aetate maximi clarissimam vitam et egregios atque moderni temporis hominibus vix imitabiles actus pati oblivionis tenebris aboleri. Suberat et

Titulus et Praefatio desunt in AB   1. 10 dissertissimis *C*

alia non inrationabilis, ut opinor, causa, quae vel sola
sufficere posset, ut me ad haec scribenda conpelleret,
nutrimentum videlicet in me inpensum et perpetua,
postquam in aula eius conversari coepi, cum ipso ac
liberis eius amicitia; qua me ita sibi devinxit debi-
toremque tam vivo quam mortuo constituit, ut merito
ingratus videri et iudicari possem, si tot beneficiorum
in me conlatorum inmemor clarissima et inlustrissima
hominis optime de me meriti gesta silentio praeterirem
patererque vitam eius, quasi qui numquam vixerit, sine
litteris ac debita laude manere. Cui scribendae atque
explicandae non meum ingeniolum, quod exile et par-
vum, immo paene nullum est, sed Tullianam par erat
desudare facundiam. En tibi librum praeclarissimi et
maximi viri memoriam continentem; in quo praeter
illius facta non est quod admireris, nisi forte, quod homo
barbarus et in Romana locutione perparum exercitatus
aliquid me decenter aut commode Latine scribere posse
putaverim atque in tantam inpudentiam proruperim, ut
illud Ciceronis putarem contemnendum, quod in primo
Tusculanarum libro, cum de Latinis scriptoribus loque-
retur, ita dixisse legitur: *Mandare quemquam,* inquit,
*litteris cogitationes suas, qui eas nec disponere nec inlu-
strare possit nec delectatione aliqua adlicere lectorem, hominis est intemperanter abutentis et otio et litteris.* Poterat
quidem haec oratoris egregii sententia me a scribendo
deterrere, nisi animo praemeditatum haberem hominum
iudicia potius experiri et haec scribendo ingenioli mei
periculum facere quam tanti viri memoriam mihi par-
cendo praeterire.

VITA KAROLI

1. Gens Meroingorum, de qua Franci reges sibi creare soliti erant, usque in Hildricum regem, qui iussu Stephani Romani pontificis depositus ac detonsus atque in monasterium trusus est, durasse putatur. Quae licet in illo finita possit videri, tamen iam dudum nullius vigoris erat, nec quicquam in se clarum praeter inane regis vocabulum praeferebat. Nam et opes et potentia regni penes palatii praefectos, qui maiores domus dicebantur, et ad quos summa imperii pertinebat, tenebantur. Neque regi aliud relinquebatur quam ut regio tantum nomine contentus crine profuso, barba summissa, solio resideret ac speciem dominantis effingeret, legatos undecumque venientes audiret eisque abeuntibus responsa, quae erat edoctus vel etiam iussus, ex sua velut potestate redderet; cum praeter inutile regis nomen et precarium vitae stipendium, quod ei praefectus aulae prout videbatur exhibebat, nihil aliud proprii possideret quam unam et eam praeparvi reditus villam, in qua domum et ex qua famulos sibi necessaria ministrantes atque obsequium exhibentes paucae numerositatis habebat. Quocumque eundum erat, carpento ibat, quod bubus iunctis et bubulco rustico more agente trahebatur. Sic ad palatium, sic ad publicum populi sui conventum, qui annuatim ob regni utilitatem celebrabatur, ire, sic domum redire solebat. At regni administrationem et omnia quae vel domi vel foris agenda ac disponenda erant praefectus aulae procurabat.

1. 1. 1 Gens Meroingorum] Incipit liber *praefixit* C   2 Hildrichum C : Childricum B   3, 4 monasterium Sithiu trusus *unus cod*.   **2.** 12 perparvi *nonnulli codd*.   **3.** 5 ad AB

2. Quo officio tum, cum Hildricus deponebatur, Pippinus pater Karoli regis iam velut hereditario fungebatur. Nam pater eius Karolus, qui tyrannos per totam Franciam dominatum sibi vindicantes oppressit et Sarracenos Galliam occupare temptantes duobus magnis proeliis, uno in Aquitania apud Pictavium civitatem, altero iuxta Narbonam apud Birram fluvium, ita devicit, ut in Hispaniam eos redire conpelleret, eundem magistratum a patre Pippino sibi dimissum egregie administravit. Qui honor non aliis a populo dari consueverat quam his qui et claritate generis et opum amplitudine ceteris eminebant.

Hunc cum Pippinus pater Karoli regis ab avo et patre sibi et fratri Karlomanno relictum, summa cum eo concordia divisum, aliquot annis velut sub rege memorato tenuisset, frater eius Karlomannus — incertum quibus de causis, tamen videtur quod amore conversationis contemplativae succensus —, operosa temporalis regni administratione relicta, Romam se in otium contulit, ibique habitu permutato monachus factus in monte Soracte apud ecclesiam beati Silvestri constructo monasterio cum fratribus secum ad hoc venientibus per aliquot annos optata quiete perfruitur. Sed cum ex Francia multi nobilium ob vota solvenda Romam sollemniter commearent et eum velut dominum quondam suum praeterire nollent, otium, quo maxime delectabatur, crebra salutatione interrumpentes, locum mutare conpellunt. Nam huiuscemodi frequentiam cum suo proposito officere vidisset, relicto monte in Samnium provinciam ad monasterium sancti Benedicti situm in castro Casino secessit et ibi quod reliquum erat temporalis vitae religiose conversando conplevit.

2. 1. 1 Hildrichus *C*   2. 2 sibi *om. B*   4 Pictavium *A* : Pectavium *BC*   3. 10 per *om. B*

3. Pippinus autem per auctoritatem Romani pontificis ex praefecto palatii rex constitutus, cum per annos XV aut eo amplius Francis solus imperaret, finito Aquitanico bello, quod contra Waifarium ducem Aquitaniae ab eo susceptum per continuos novem annos gerebatur, apud Parisios morbo aquae intercutis diem obiit, superstitibus liberis Karolo et Karlomanno, ad quos successio regni divino nutu pervenerat. Franci siquidem facto sollemniter generali conventu ambos sibi reges constituunt, ea conditione praemissa, ut totum regni corpus ex aequo partirentur, et Karolus eam partem quam pater eorum Pippinus tenuerat, Karlomannus vero eam cui patruus eorum Karlomannus praeerat, regendi gratia susciperet. Susceptae sunt utrimque conditiones, et pars regni divisi iuxta modum sibi propositum ab utroque recepta est. Mansitque ista, quamvis cum summa difficultate, concordia, multis ex parte Karlomanni societatem separare molientibus, adeo ut quidam eos etiam bello committere sint meditati. Sed in hoc plus suspecti quam periculi fuisse ipse rerum exitus adprobavit, cum defuncto Karlomanno uxor eius et filii cum quibusdam, qui ex optimatum eius numero primores erant, Italiam fuga petiit et nullis existentibus causis, spreto mariti fratre, sub Desiderii regis Langobardorum patrocinium se cum liberis suis contulit. Et Karlomannus quidem post administratum communiter biennio regnum morbo decessit; Karolus autem fratre defuncto consensu omnium Francorum rex constituitur.

4. De cuius nativitate atque infantia vel etiam pueritia quia neque scriptis usquam aliquid declaratum est, neque quisquam modo superesse invenitur qui horum

---

3. 1. 7 Karlo *ABC*   2. 5, 6 vero ... Karlomannus *om. B*
3. 1 suscepti *C*   9 *Post* eius *add.* quae dicitur Teoberga *unus cod.*   4. 2 communi(ter *sscr.*) *A*   **4.** 1. 2 umquam *B*

se dicat habere notitiam, scribere ineptum iudicans ad
actus et mores ceterasque vitae illius partes explicandas
ac demonstrandas, omissis incognitis, transire disposui ;
ita tamen ut primo res gestas et domi et foris, deinde
mores et studia eius, tum de regni administratione et
fine narrando nihil de his quae cognitu vel digna vel
necessaria sunt praetermittam.

5. Omnium bellorum quae gessit, primo Aquitanicum,
a patre inchoatum, sed nondum finitum, quia cito peragi
posse videbatur, fratre adhuc vivo, etiam et auxilium
ferre rogato, suscepit. Et licet eum frater promisso
frustrasset auxilio, susceptam expeditionem strenuissime
exsecutus non prius incepto desistere aut semel suscepto
labori cedere voluit, quam hoc quod efficere moliebatur
perseverantia quadam ac iugitate perfecto fine conclu-
deret. Nam et Hunoldum, qui post Waifarii mortem
Aquitaniam occupare bellumque iam paene peractum
reparare temptaverat, Aquitaniam relinquere et Wasconiam petere coegit. Quem tamen ibi consistere non
sustinens, transmisso amne Garonna, Lupo Wasconum
duci per legatos mandat ut perfugam reddat ; quod ni
festinato faciat, bello se eum expostulaturum. Sed
Lupus saniori usus consilio non solum Hunoldum reddidit, sed etiam se ipsum cum provincia cui praeerat
eius potestati permisit.

6. Conpositis in Aquitania rebus eoque bello finito,
regni quoque socio iam rebus humanis exempto, rogatu
et precibus Hadriani Romanae urbis episcopi exoratus
bellum contra Langobardos suscepit. Quod prius quidem
et a patre eius, Stephano papa supplicante, cum magna

2. 4 sunt *om. B*   **5.** 1. 4 fratre *B*¹   7 quam] quia (*ex*
qua *corr.*) *A*   2. 2 poene *ABC, ut ubique*   5 *Post* Garonna
add. et aedificato castro Frontiaco *unus cod.*   6 ut *om. C*
10 potestate *B*   **6.** 1. 3 Adriani *B*   4 Longobardos *A*
5 stefano *C*

difficultate susceptum est ; quia quidam e primoribus
Francorum, cum quibus consultare solebat, adeo voluntati eius renisi sunt, ut se regem deserturos domumque
redituros libera voce proclamarent. Susceptum tamen
est tunc contra Haistulfum regem et celerrime conpletum. Sed licet sibi et patri belli suscipiendi similis **2**
ac potius eadem causa subesse videretur, haud simili
tamen et labore certatum et fine constat esse conpletum.
Pippinus siquidem Haistulfum regem paucorum dierum
obsidione apud Ticenum conpulit et obsides dare et
erepta Romanis oppida atque cestella restituere atque,
ut reddita non repeterentur, sacramento fidem facere ;
Karolus vero post inchoatum a se bellum non prius
destitit quam et Desiderium regem, quem longa obsidione
fatigaverat, in deditionem susciperet, filium eius Adal-
gisum, in quem spes omnium inclinatae videbantur, non
solum regno sed etiam Italia excedere conpelleret, omnia
Romanis erepta restitueret, Hruodgausum Foroiuliani
ducatus praefectum res novas molientem opprimeret
totamque Italiam suae ditioni subiugaret subactaeque
filium suum Pippinum regem inponeret. Italiam intranti **3**
quam difficilis Alpium transitus fuerit, quantoque Francorum labore invia montium iuga et eminentes in caelum
scopuli atque asperae cautes superatae sint, hoc loco
describerem, nisi vitae illius modum potius quam bellorum quae gessit eventus memoriae mandare praesenti
opere animo esset propositum. Finis tamen huius belli **4**
fuit subacta Italia et rex Desiderius perpetuo exilio
deportatus et filius eius Adalgisus Italia pulsus et res
a Langobardorum regibus ereptae Hadriano Romanae
ecclesiae rectori restitutae.

6 est *om. B*   quidam *ex* quadam *corr. A*   2. 1 et] ac *B*
4 Aistulfum *B*   8 Karolus *B* : Karlus *AC*   11 inclite *B*
4. 4 Longobardorum *B*

7. Post cuius finem Saxonicum, quod quasi intermissum videbatur, repetitum est. Quo nullum neque prolixius neque atrocius Francorumque populo laboriosius susceptum est; quia Saxones, sicut omnes fere Germaniam incolentes nationes, et natura feroces et cultui daemonum dediti nostraeque religioni contrarii neque divina neque humana iura vel polluere vel transgredi inhonestum arbitrabantur. Suberant et causae quae cotidie pacem conturbare poterant, termini videlicet nostri et illorum paene ubique in plano contigui, praeter pauca loca, in quibus vel silvae maiores vel montium iuga interiecta utrorumque agros certo limite disterminant, in quibus caedes et rapinae et incendia vicissim fieri non cessabant. Quibus adeo Franci sunt irritati ut non iam vicissitudinem reddere, sed apertum contra eos bellum suscipere dignum iudicarent. Susceptum est igitur adversus eos bellum, quod magna utrimque animositate, tamen maiore Saxonum quam Francorum damno, per continuos triginta tres annos gerebatur. Poterat siquidem citius finiri, si Saxonum hoc perfidia pateretur. Difficile dictu est, quoties superati ac supplices regi se dediderunt, imperata facturos polliciti sunt, obsides qui imperabantur absque dilatione dederunt, legatos qui mittebantur susceperunt, aliquoties ita domiti et emolliti ut etiam cultum daemonum dimittere et Christianae religioni se subdere velle promitterent. Sed sicut ad haec facienda aliquoties proni, sic ad eadem pervertenda semper fuere praecipites, ut non sit satis aestimare ad utrum horum faciliores verius dici possint; quippe cum post inchoatum cum eis bellum vix ullus annus exactus sit, quo non ab eis huiuscemodi facta sit permutatio. Sed magnanimitas regis ac perpetua tam

7. 2. 7 ideo *B*   3. 1 dictum *B*   4. 2 ut non sit *dett. nonnulli*: non sit ut *ABC*

in adversis quam in prosperis mentis constantia nulla eorum mutabilitate vel vinci poterat vel ab his quae agere coeperat defatigari. Nam numquam eos huiuscemodi aliquid perpetrantes inpune ferre passus est, quin aut ipse per se ducto aut per comites suos misso exercitu perfidiam ulcisceretur et dignam ab eis poenam exigeret, usque dum, omnibus qui resistere solebant profligatis et in suam potestatem redactis, decem milia hominum ex his qui utrasque ripas Albis fluminis incolebant cum uxoribus et parvulis sublatos transtulit et huc atque illuc per Galliam et Germaniam multimoda divisione distribuit. Eaque conditione a rege proposita et ab illis suscepta tractum per tot annos bellum constat esse finitum, ut, abiecto daemonum cultu et relictis patriis caerimoniis, Christianae fidei atque religionis sacramenta susciperent et Francis adunati unus cum eis populus efficerentur.

8. Hoc bello, licet per multum temporis spatium traheretur, ipse non amplius cum hoste quam bis acie conflixit, semel iuxta montem qui Osneggi dicitur in loco Theotmelli nominato et iterum apud Hasam fluvium, et hoc uno mense, paucis quoque interpositis diebus. His duobus proeliis hostes adeo profligati ac devicti sunt ut ulterius regem neque provocare neque venienti resistere, nisi aliqua loci munitione defensi, auderent. Plures tamen eo bello tam ex nobilitate Francorum quam Saxonum et functi summis honoribus viri consumpti sunt. Tandemque anno tricesimo tertio finitum est, cum interim tot ac tanta in diversis terrarum partibus bella contra Francos et exorta sint et sollertia regis administrata ut merito intuentibus in dubium venire possit, utrum in eo aut laborum patientiam aut felici-

---

5. 4 perfidiam eorum ulcisceretur *C*   6 redactis *om. A*
6. 5 *Fort.* adiuncti   **8.** 1. 4 Hasam *C* : Hasa *AB*

tatem potius mirari conveniat. Nam biennio ante Italicum hoc bellum sumpsit exordium, et cum sine intermissione gereretur, nihil tamen ex his quae aliubi erant gerenda dimissum aut ulla in parte ab aeque operoso certamine cessatum est. Nam rex, omnium qui sua aetate gentibus dominabantur et prudentia maximus et animi magnitudine praestantissimus, nihil in his quae vel suscipienda erant vel exsequenda aut propter laborem detrectavit aut propter periculum exhorruit, verum unumquodque secundum suam qualitatem et subire et ferre doctus nec [in] adversis cedere nec in prosperis falso blandienti fortunae adsentiri solebat.

9. Cum enim assiduo ac paene continuo cum Saxonibus bello certaretur, dispositis per congrua confiniorum loca praesidiis, Hispaniam quam maximo poterat belli apparatu adgreditur; saltuque Pyrinei superato, omnibus quae adierat oppidis atque castellis in deditionem acceptis, salvo et incolomi exercitu revertitur; praeter quod in ipso Pyrinei iugo Wasconicam perfidiam parumper in redeundo contigit experiri. Nam cum agmine longo, ut loci et angustiarum situs permittebat, porrectus iret exercitus, Wascones in summi montis vertice positis insidiis — est enim locus ex opacitate silvarum, quarum ibi maxima est copia, insidiis ponendis oportunus — extremam impedimentorum partem et eos qui novissimi agminis incedentes subsidio praecedentes tuebantur desuper incursantes in subiectam vallem deiciunt, consertoque cum eis proelio usque ad unum omnes interficiunt, ac direptis impedimentis, noctis beneficio quae iam instabat protecti summa cum celeritate in diversa disperguntur. Adiuvabat in hoc facto Wascones et levitas armorum et loci in quo res gerebatur situs, econtra

3. 9 detractavit *A*   11 in *ABC*: *seclusimus*   **9**. 1. 7 parumper *om. C*   2. 4 quarum ibi *om. B*   3. 2 econtra] et contra *B*

Francos et armorum gravitas et loci iniquitas per omnia Wasconibus reddidit impares. In quo proelio Eggihardus regiae mensae praepositus, Anshelmus comes palatii et Hruodlandus Brittannici limitis praefectus cum aliis conpluribus interficiuntur. Neque hoc factum ad praesens vindicari poterat, quia hostis re perpetrata ita dispersus est ut ne fama quidem remaneret ubinam gentium quaeri potuisset.

10. Domuit et Brittones, qui ad occidentem in extrema quadam parte Galliae super litus oceani residentes dicto audientes non erant, missa in eos expeditione, qua et obsides dare et quae imperarentur se facturos polliceri coacti sunt. Ipse postea cum exercitu Italiam ingressus ac per Romam iter agens Capuam Campaniae urbem accessit atque ibi positis castris bellum Beneventanis, ni dederentur, comminatus est. Praevenit hoc dux gentis Aragisus: filios suos Rumoldum et Grimoldum cum magna pecunia obviam regi mittens rogat ut filios obsides suscipiat, seque cum gente imperata facturum pollicetur, praeter hoc solum, si ipse ad conspectum venire cogeretur. Rex, utilitate gentis magis quam animi eius obstinatione considerata, et oblatos sibi obsides suscepit eique ut ad conspectum venire non cogeretur pro magno munere concessit; unoque ex filiis, qui minor erat, obsidatus gratia retento, maiorem patri remisit; legatisque ob sacramenta fidelitatis a Beneventanis exigenda atque suscipienda cum Aragiso dimissis Romam redit, consumptisque ibi in sanctorum veneratione locorum aliquot diebus in Galliam revertitur.

11. Baioaricum deinde bellum et repente ortum et celeri fine conpletum est. Quod superbia simul ac

6 et Hruodlandus Brittannici limitis praefectus *om. B*
10. 2. 5 Romoldum cum (et Grimoldum *om.*) *B*   3. 3 ut *om. B*
9 aliquod *B*

socordia Tassilonis ducis excitavit, qui hortatu uxoris, quae filia Desiderii regis erat ac patris exilium per maritum ulcisci posse putabat, iuncto foedere cum Hunis, qui Baioariis sunt ab oriente contermini, non solum imperata non facere sed bello regem provocare temptabat. Cuius contumaciam, quia nimia videbatur, animositas regis ferre nequiverat, ac proinde copiis undique contractis Baioariam petiturus ipse ad Lechum amnem cum magno venit exercitu. Is fluvius Baioarios ab Alamannis dividit. Cuius in ripa castris conlocatis, priusquam provinciam intraret animum ducis per legatos statuit experiri. Sed nec ille pertinaciter agere vel sibi vel genti utile ratus supplex se regi permisit, obsides qui imperabantur dedit, inter quos et filium suum Theodonem, data insuper fide cum iuramento, quod ab illius potestate ad defectionem nemini suadenti adsentiri deberet. Sicque bello, quod quasi maximum futurum videbatur, celerrimus est finis inpositus. Tassilo tamen postmodum ad regem evocatus neque redire permissus ; neque provincia quam tenebat ulterius duci, sed comitibus ad regendum commissa est.

12. His motibus ita conpositis, Sclavis, qui nostra consuetudine Wilzi, proprie vero, id est sua locutione, Welatabi dicuntur, bellum inlatum est. In quo et Saxones velut auxiliares inter ceteras nationes quae regis signa iussae sequebantur, quamquam ficta et minus devota oboedientia, militabant. Causa belli erat quod Abodritos, qui cum Francis olim foederati erant, adsidua incursione lacessebant nec iussionibus coerceri poterant.

11. 1. 4 patris] *fort.* fratris ; *cf. tamen* **6.** 4. 2 *et* **19.** 2. 10 *et Ann. Einh. sub anno* 788   5 posse *om. B*   2. 1 quae nima *B*   4 magno *C*: maximo *AB*   venit *om. B*   7 statuit *om. B*   3. 5 nullo *B* adsentiri *C*: adsentire *AB*   **12.** 1. 2 id est sua locutione] *fort. secludendum* ; *cf.* **29.** 3. 1–4   3 et *om. A*   4 auxiliares *A* : auxiares *B* : auxiliatores *C*   2. 3 lacessebant *B* : lacescebant *AC*

Sinus quidam ab occidentali oceano orientem versus porrigitur, longitudinis quidem inconpertae, latitudinis vero quae nusquam centum milia passuum excedat, cum in multis locis contractior inveniatur. Hunc multae circumsedent nationes. Dani siquidem ac Sueones, quos Nordmannos vocamus, et septentrionale litus et omnes in eo insulas tenent. At litus australe Sclavi et Aisti et aliae diversae incolunt nationes; inter quos vel praecipui sunt, quibus tunc a rege bellum inferebatur, Welatabi. Quos ille una tantum et quam per se gesserat expeditione ita contudit ac domuit ut ulterius imperata facere minime renuendum iudicarent.

13. Maximum omnium quae ab illo gesta sunt bellorum praeter Saxonicum huic bello successit, illud videlicet quod contra Avares sive Hunos susceptum est. Quod ille et animosius quam cetera et longe maiori apparatu administravit. Unam tamen per se in Pannoniam — nam hanc provinciam ea gens tum incolebat — expeditionem fecit, cetera filio suo Pippino ac praefectis provinciarum, comitibus etiam atque legatis perficienda commisit. Quod cum ab his strenuissime fuisset administratum, octavo tandem anno conpletum est. Quot proelia in eo gesta, quantum sanguinis effusum sit, testatur vacua omni habitatore Pannonia et locus in quo regia Kagani erat ita desertus ut ne vestigium quidem in eo humanae habitationis appareat. Tota in hoc bello Hunorum nobilitas periit, tota gloria decidit. Omnis pecunia et congesti ex longo tempore thesauri direpti sunt. Neque ullum bellum contra Francos exortum humana potest memoria recordari quo illi magis ditati et opibus aucti sint. Quippe cum usque in id

---

3. 3 Nordmannos *AB* : Nortmannos *C*   4 ad *B, fort. recte*
13. 1. 3 auros sive unos *B*   2. 6 hoc *om. B*   honorum (*corr. ex* horum) *B*   3. 3 sunt *B*

temporis paene pauperes viderentur, tantum auri et argenti in regia repertum, tot spolia pretiosa in proeliis sublata, ut merito credi possit hoc Francos Hunis iuste eripuisse quod Huni prius aliis gentibus iniuste eripuerunt. Duo tantum ex proceribus Francorum eo bello perierunt : Ericus dux Foroiulianus in Liburnia iuxta Tharsaticam maritimam civitatem insidiis oppidanorum interceptus, et Geroldus Baioariae praefectus in Pannonia, cum contra Hunos proeliaturus aciem strueret, incertum a quo, cum duobus tantum, qui eum obequitantem ac singulos hortantem comitabantur, interfectus est. Ceterum incruentum paene Francis hoc bellum fuit et prosperrimum exitum habuit, tametsi diutius sui magnitudine traheretur. Post quod et Saxonicum suae prolixitati convenientem finem accepit. Boemanicum quoque et Linonicum, quae postea exorta sunt, diu durare non potuerunt ; quorum utrumque ductu Karoli iunioris celeri fine conpletum est.

14. Ultimum contra Nordmannos qui Dani vocantur, primo pyraticam exercentes, deinde maiori classe litora Galliae atque Germaniae vastantes, bellum susceptum est. Quorum rex Godofridus adeo vana spe inflatus erat ut sibi totius Germaniae promitteret potestatem. Frisiam quoque atque Saxoniam haud aliter atque suas provincias aestimabat. Iam Abodritos, vicinos suos, in suam ditionem redegerat, iam eos sibi vectigales fecerat : iactabat etiam se brevi Aquasgrani, ubi regis comitatus erat, cum maximis copiis adventurum. Nec dictis eius, quamvis vanissimis, omnino fides abnuebatur, quin potius putaretur tale aliquid inchoaturus, nisi festinata

---

4. 2 Foriiulianus *B* : Forojulanus *AC*   3 tharasaticam (*corr. ex* thras-) *B*   4 interceptus *B* : intercoeptus *A* : inter ceptum *C*   8 est] *om. unus det., fort. secludendum*   **14.** 1. 1 Nordmannos *AB* : Nortmannos *C*   2. 3 *prius* atque *om. B*   6 cominatus *B*

VITA KAROLI

fuisset morte praeventus. Nam a proprio satellite interfectus et suae vitae et belli a se inchoati finem acceleravit.

15. Haec sunt bella, quae rex potentissimus per annos XLVII — tot enim annis regnaverat — in diversis terrarum partibus summa prudentia atque felicitate gessit : quibus regnum Francorum, quod post patrem Pippinum magnum quidem et forte susceperat, ita nobiliter ampliavit ut paene duplum illi adiecerit. Nam cum prius non amplius quam ea pars Galliae quae inter Rhenum et Ligerim oceanumque ac mare Balearicum iacet, et pars Germaniae, quae inter Saxoniam et Danubium Rhenumque ac Salam fluvium, qui Thuringos et Sorabos dividit, posita a Francis qui orientales dicuntur incolitur, et praeter haec Alamanni atque Baioarii ad regni Francorum potestatem pertinerent : ipse per bella memorata primo Aquitaniam et Wasconiam totumque Pyrinei montis iugum et usque ad Hiberum amnem, qui apud Navarros ortus et fertilissimos Hispaniae agros secans sub Dertosae civitatis moenibus Balearico mari miscetur ; deinde Italiam totam, quae ab Augusta Praetoria usque in Calabriam inferiorem (in qua Graecorum ac Beneventanorum constat esse confinia) decies centum et eo amplius passuum milibus longitudine porrigitur ; tum Saxoniam, quae quidem Germaniae pars non modica est et eius quae a Francis incolitur duplum in lato habere putatur, cum ei longitudine possit esse consimilis ; post quam utramque Pannoniam et adpositam in altera Danubii ripa Daciam, Histriam quoque et Liburniam atque Dalmaciam, exceptis maritimis civitatibus, quas ob amicitiam et iunctum cum eo foedus Constantino-

15. 1. 4 Pippini *C*   2. 2 qua *C*   3 Ligerim *C* : Ligerem *AB*   5 Thuringos *B* : Turingos *A* : Thuringo *C*   3. 2 Equitaniam *B*   5 moenibus *C* : moenia *AB*   4. 1 quamque *B* positam *B*   2 historiam *C*   3, 4 exceptis... amicitiam *om. B*

politanum imperatorem habere permisit ; deinde omnes barbaras ac feras nationes, quae inter Rhenum ac Visulam fluvios oceanumque ac Danubium positae, lingua quidem paene similes, moribus vero atque habitu valde dissimiles, Germaniam incolunt, ita perdomuit ut eas tributarias efficeret ; inter quas fere praecipuae sunt Welatabi, Sorabi, Abodriti, Boemani ; cum his namque bello conflixit, ceteras, quarum multo maior est numerus, in deditionem suscepit.

16. Auxit etiam gloriam regni sui quibusdam regibus ac gentibus per amicitiam sibi conciliatis. Adeo namque Hadefonsum Galleciae atque Asturicae regem sibi societate devinxit ut is, cum ad eum vel litteras vel legatos mitteret, non aliter se apud illum quam proprium suum appellari iuberet. Scottorum quoque reges sic habuit ad suam voluntatem per munificentiam inclinatos ut eum numquam aliter nisi dominum seque subditos et servos eius pronuntiarent. Extant epistolae ab eis ad illum missae, quibus huiusmodi affectus eorum erga illum indicatur. Cum Aaron rege Persarum, qui excepta India totum paene tenebat orientem, talem habuit in amicitia concordiam ut is gratiam eius omnium, qui in toto orbe terrarum erant, regum ac principum amicitiae praeponeret solumque illum honore ac munificentia sibi colendum iudicaret. Ac proinde, cum legati eius, quos cum donariis ad sacratissimum Domini ac salvatoris nostri sepulchrum locumque resurrectionis miserat, ad eum venissent et ei domini sui voluntatem indicassent, non solum quae petebantur fieri permisit, sed etiam sacrum illum et salutarem locum, ut illius potestati adscriberetur, concessit ; et revertentibus legatis suos

---

5. 6 tributarios *B* **16.** 1. 3 Ahdefonsum Galleciae atque Austricae *B* 4 is *om. B* **2.** 1 Scotorum *B* 5 effectus *A* **3.** 4 amicitia *B* 12 adscriberetur, non cessit *C*

VITA KAROLI

adiungens inter vestes et aromata et ceteras orientalium terrarum opes ingentia illi dona direxit, cum ei ante paucos annos eum quem tunc solum habebat roganti mitteret elephantum. Imperatores etiam Constantinopolitani, Nicephorus, Michahel et Leo, ultro amicitiam et societatem eius expetentes conplures ad eum misere legatos. Cum quibus tamen propter susceptum a se imperatoris nomen et ob hoc, quasi qui imperium eis eripere vellet, valde suspectum, foedus firmissimum statuit, ut nulla inter partes cuiuslibet scandali remaneret occasio. Erat enim semper Romanis et Graecis Francorum suspecta potentia. Unde et illud Graecum extat proverbium: ΤΟΝ ΦΡΑΝΚΟΝ ΦΙΛΟΝ ΕΞΕΙΣ, ΓΕΙΤΟΝΑ ΟΥΚ ΕΞΕΙΣ

17. Qui cum tantus in ampliando regno et subigendis exteris nationibus existeret et in eiusmodi occupationibus assidue versaretur, opera tamen plurima ad regni decorem et commoditatem pertinentia diversis in locis inchoavit, quaedam etiam consummavit. Inter quae praecipua non inmerito videri possunt basilica sanctae Dei genitricis Aquisgrani opere mirabili constructa et pons apud Mogontiacum in Rheno quingentorum passuum longitudinis — nam tanta est ibi fluminis latitudo; qui tamen uno, antequam decederet, anno incendio conflagravit, nec refici potuit propter festinatum illius decessum, quamquam in ea meditatione esset ut pro ligneo lapideum restitueret. Inchoavit et palatia operis egregii, unum haud longe a Mogontiaco civitate, iuxta villam cui vocabulum est Ingilenheim, alterum

---

16 elefantum *ABC*   4. 2 Niciforus *C*: Nicifuorus *B*: Nuciforus *A*   5 hoc eis quasi *B*   6 susceptum *A*   9 suscepta *A*   10, 11 ΕΞΙC *ABC* (*bis*)   ΓΙΤΟΝΑ *C*: ΤΙΤΟΝΑ *A*: ΓΙΤΟΝΑ ΟΥΚ ΕΞΙC *om. B*   17. 2. 2 praecipua] praecipua fore *B*: praecipua fere *multi codd.*   5 longitudini *C*   nam *om. B*   7 nec *AB*: nam *C*   3. 2 Magontiam *B*   3 cuius *A*

Noviomagi super Vahalem fluvium, qui Batavorum insulam a parte meridiana praeterfluit. Praecipue tamen aedes sacras ubicumque in toto regno suo vetustate conlapsas conperit, pontificibus et patribus, ad quorum curam pertinebant, ut restaurarentur imperavit, adhibens curam per legatos ut imperata perficerent.
4 Molitus est et classem contra bellum Norðmannicum, aedificatis ad hoc navibus iuxta flumina quae et de Gallia et de Germania septentrionalem influunt oceanum. Et quia Norðmanni Gallicum litus atque Germanicum 5 assidua infestatione vastabant, per omnes portus et ostia fluminum, qua naves recipi posse videbantur, stationibus et excubiis dispositis, ne qua hostis exire potuisset tali munitione prohibuit. Fecit idem a parte meridiana in litore provinciae Narbonensis ac Septi-10 maniae, toto etiam Italiae litore usque Romam contra Mauros nuper pyraticam exercere adgressos ; ac per hoc nullo gravi damno vel a Mauris Italia vel Gallia atque Germania a Norðmannis diebus suis adfecta est, praeter quod Centumcellae civitas Etruriae per proditionem 15 a Mauris capta atque vastata est, et in Frisia quaedam insulae Germanico litori contiguae a Norðmannis depraedatae sunt.

18. Talem eum in tuendo et ampliando simulque ornando regno fuisse constat. Cuius animi dotes et summam in qualicumque et prospero et adverso eventu constantiam ceteraque ad interiorem atque domesticam 5 vitam pertinentia iam abhinc dicere exordiar.

2 Post mortem patris cum fratre regnum partitus tanta patientia simultates et invidiam eius tulit, ut omnibus

---

7 pontifici *C*   8 restauremtur *B*   4. 1 Nordmannicum *BC* : Nordomannicum *A*   4 Norðmanni *C* : Nordmanni *A* : Nordomanni *B*   5 infestatione *A* : infestinatione *BC*   11 adgressus *B*   13 affecta *A*   16 Nordmannis *AC* : Nordomannis *B*   **18.** 1. 3 quacumque *A*   4 cetera quae *Bb*

VITA KAROLI

mirum videretur quod ne ad iracundiam quidem ab eo provocari potuisset. Deinde cum matris hortatu filiam Desiderii regis Langobardorum duxisset uxorem, incertum qua de causa, post annum eam repudiavit et Hildigardam de gente Suaborum, praecipuae nobilitatis feminam, in matrimonium accepit; de qua tres filios, Karolum videlicet, Pippinum et Hludowicum, totidemque filias, Hruodtrudem et Berhtam et Gislam, genuit. Habuit et alias tres filias, Theoderadam et Hiltrudem **3** et Hruodhaidem, duas de Fastrada uxore, quae de orientalium Francorum, Germanorum videlicet, gente erat, tertiam de concubina quadam, cuius nomen modo memoriae non occurrit. Defuncta Fastrada Liutgardam 5 Alamannam duxit, de qua nihil liberorum tulit: post cuius mortem quattuor habuit concubinas, Madelgardam scilicet, quae peperit ei filiam nomine Ruothildem, Gersuindam Saxonici generis, de qua ei filia [nomen] Adaltrud nata est, et Reginam, quae ei Drogonem et 10 Hugum genuit, et Adallindem, ex qua Theodericum procreavit. Mater quoque eius Berhtrada in magno **4** apud eum honore consenuit. Colebat enim eam cum summa reverentia, ita ut nulla umquam invicem sit exorta discordia, praeter in divortio filiae Desiderii regis quam illa suadente acceperat. Decessit tandem post 5 mortem Hildigardae, cum iam tres nepotes suos toti-

2. 3 nec *b*   6 et *om. b*   7 Hildigardam *C*: Hildigardem *AB*: Hildegardem *b*   Suahorum *C*   9 Hludowicum *Ab*: Hludoicum *BC*   10 Hruodtrudem *B*: Hruadrudem *b*: Hruodrudem *A*: Hruotrudem *C*   Bertham *b*   Gisalam *b*
3. 2 Ruadhaidem *b*   4 connubia *b*   5 Leutgardem *B*   6 liberum nihil *b*   7 quattuor *C*: tres *ABb*   7, 8 Madelgardam ... Ruothildem *habet C, om. ABb*   9 Gersuuindam *b*   ei *ABb*: illi *C*   nomen *ABb*: nomine *C*: *seclusimus*   11 et *om. B*
   Adallindem *AC*: Adallindam *b*: Adaltrudem *B*   Theodricum *b*   4. 1 Berhtrada *A*: Brethrada *BbC*   5 susceperat *b*   decessitque *C*: discessit *b*   6 Hildegardae *b*

demque neptis in filii domo vidisset. Quam ille in eadem basilica qua pater situs est, apud Sanctum Dionysium, magno cum honore fecit humari. Erat ei unica soror nomine Gisla, a puellaribus annis religiosae conversationi mancipata, quam similiter ut matrem magna coluit pietate. Quae etiam paucis ante obitum illius annis in eo quo conversata est monasterio decessit.

19. Liberos suos ita censuit instituendos ut tam filii quam filiae primo liberalibus studiis, quibus et ipse operam dabat, erudirentur: tum filios, cum primum aetas patiebatur, more Francorum equitare, armis ac venatibus exerceri fecit, filias vero lanificio adsuescere coloque ac fuso, ne per otium torperent, operam impendere atque ad omnem honestatem erudiri iussit.

Ex his omnibus duos tantum filios et unam filiam, priusquam moreretur, amisit, Karolum, qui natu maior erat, et Pippinum, quem regem Italiae praefecerat, et Hruodtrudem, quae filiarum eius primogenita et a Constantino Grecorum imperatore desponsata erat. Quorum Pippinus unum filium suum Bernhardum, filias autem quinque, Adalhaidem, Atulam, Gundradam, Berhthaidem ac Theoderadam, superstites reliquit. In quibus rex pietatis suae praecipuum documentum ostendit, cum filio defuncto nepotem patri succedere et neptes inter filias suas educari fecisset. Mortes filiorum ac filiae pro magnanimitate, qua excellebat, minus patienter tulit,

---

7 neptis *B* : neptes *AbC*   8 Dionisium *BC* : Dyonisium *Ab*
9 cum *om. A*   **19.** 1. 1 ita *ABC* : ante *b*   5 venationibus *B*   6 fusio *A*   7 erudire *b*   2. 2 moreretur *C* : moriretur *ABb*   4 Hruodtrudem *B* : Hruodrudem *A* : Hruothrudem *b* : Hruodthrudem *C*   5 desponsata *AC* : disponsata *Bb*   6 unicum *b*   7 Adalheidem *b*   Gundratam *b*   Berthaidem *A* : Berthaidem *C* : Berthaidam *B* : Perthaidam *b*   8 Theoderatam *b*   reliquid *B*   10 patri *C* : patris *AB* : fratris *b*   et neptes *A* : et neptas *b* : et nectes *C* : *om. B*
3. 2 quae *BC*

VITA KAROLI

pietate videlicet, qua non minus insignis erat, conpulsus ad lacrimas. Nuntiato etiam sibi Hadriani Romani pontificis obitu, quem in amicis praecipuum habebat, sic flevit ac si fratrem aut karissimum filium amisisset. Erat enim in amicitiis optime temperatus, ut eas et facile admitteret et constantissime retineret, colebatque sanctissime quoscumque hac adfinitate sibi coniunxerat. Filiorum ac filiarum tantam in educando curam habuit, ut numquam domi positus sine ipsis cenaret, numquam iter sine illis faceret. Adequitabant ei filii, filiae vero pone sequebantur, quarum agmen extremum ex satellitum numero ad hoc ordinati tuebantur. Quae cum pulcherrimae essent et ab eo plurimum diligerentur, mirum dictu quod nullam earum cuiquam aut suorum aut exterorum nuptum dare voluit, sed omnes secum usque ad obitum suum in domo sua retinuit, dicens se earum contubernio carere non posse. [Ac propter hoc, licet alias felix, adversae fortunae malignitatem expertus est. Quod tamen ita dissimulavit ac si de eis nulla umquam alicuius probri suspicio exorta vel fama dispersa fuisset.]

20. Erat ei filius nomine Pippinus ex concubina editus, cuius inter ceteros mentionem facere distuli, facie quidem pulcher, sed gibbo deformis. Is, cum pater bello contra Hunos suscepto in Baioaria hiemaret, aegritudine simulata cum quibusdam e primoribus Francorum, qui eum vana regni promissione inlexerant, adversus patrem coniuravit. Quem post fraudem detectam et coniuratorum damnationem detonsum in coenobio Prumia religiosae

---

4 Adriani *b*.   6 ac sic *B*   aut] an *B*   karissimum *C* : carissimum *ABb*   7 enim *AbC* : autem *B*   9 ac *Bb*   sibi om. *B*   4. 1 tantum *Bb*   3 faciebat *b*   4 paene *b* 9 retinuit *b* : retenuit *AC* : rennuit *B*   5. 1–4 Ac ... fuisset *habent ABb* : *om. C, seclusimus*   **20.** 1. 3 gypbo *b* 7 coniuratorum damnationem detonsum *C* : damnationem coniuratorum detonsum *Bb* : detonsum coniuratorum et damnationem *A*   8 coenobio *A* : coenubio *C* : coenobium *B* : cenubii *b*

vitae iamque volentem vacare permisit. Facta est et alia prius contra eum in Germania valida coniuratio. Cuius auctores partim luminibus orbati, partim membris incolumes, omnes tamen exilio deportati sunt; neque ullus ex eis est interfectus nisi tres tantum, qui cum se, ne conprehenderentur, strictis gladiis defenderent, aliquos etiam occidissent, quia aliter coerceri non poterant, interempti sunt. Harum tamen coniurationum Fastradae reginae crudelitas causa et origo extitisse creditur. Et idcirco in ambabus contra regem conspiratum est, quia uxoris crudelitati consentiens a suae naturae benignitate ac solita mansuetudine inmaniter exorbitasse videbatur. Ceterum per omne vitae suae tempus ita cum summo omnium amore atque favore et domi et foris conversatus est, ut numquam ei vel minima iniustae severitatis nota a quoquam fuisset obiecta.

21. Amabat peregrinos et in eis suscipiendis magnam habebat curam, adeo ut eorum multitudo non solum palatio verum etiam regno non inmerito videretur onerosa. Ipse tamen prae magnitudine animi huiuscemodi pondere minime gravabatur, cum etiam ingentia incommoda laude liberalitatis ac bonae famae mercede conpensaret.

22. Corpore fuit amplo atque robusto, statura eminenti, quae tamen iustam non excederet—nam septem suorum pedum proceritatem eius constat habuisse mensuram —, apice capitis rotundo, oculis praegrandibus ac vegetis, naso paululum mediocritatem excedenti, canitie pulchra, facie laeta et hilari; unde formae auctoritas ac dignitas tam stanti quam sedenti plurima adquirebatur;

2. 4 incolomes *ABbc*   5 tres] III (*ex* hi *corr.*) *b*   3. 2 crudelitatis *b*   4 quia *om.* B   crudelitati *AC*: crudelitate *Bb*   9 severitatis *C*: crudelitatis *ABb*   **21.** 1. 1 ac amabat *B*   2. 1 pro *unus cod.*   **22.** 1. 2 iustum non excederet modum *C*   5 paulolum *b*   canitie *b*

quamquam cervix obesa et brevior venterque proiectior videretur, tamen haec ceterorum membrorum celabat aequalitas; incessu firmo totaque corporis habitudine 3 virili; voce clara quidem, sed quae minus corporis formae conveniret; valitudine prospera, praeter quod, antequam decederet, per quatuor annos crebro febribus corripiebatur, ad extremum etiam uno pede claudicaret. 5 Et tunc quidem plura suo arbitratu quam medicorum 4 consilio faciebat, quos paene exosos habebat, quod ei in cibis assa, quibus assuetus erat, dimittere et elixis adsuescere suadebant.

Exercebatur assidue equitando ac venando; quod illi 5 gentilicium erat, quia vix ulla in terris natio invenitur quae in hac arte Francis possit aequari. Delectabatur etiam vaporibus aquarum naturaliter calentium, frequenti natatu corpus exercens; cuius adeo peritus fuit 5 ut nullus ei iuste valeat anteferri. Ob hoc etiam Aquisgrani regiam exstruxit ibique extremis vitae annis usque ad obitum perpetim habitavit. Et non solum filios ad balneum, verum optimates et amicos, aliquando etiam satellitum et custodum corporis turbam invitavit, ita 10 ut nonnumquam centum vel eo amplius homines una lavarentur.

23. Vestitu patrio, id est Francico, utebatur. Ad corpus camisam lineam, et feminalibus lineis induebatur, deinde tunicam, quae limbo serico ambiebatur, et tibialia; tum fasciolis crura et pedes calciamentis constringebat et ex pellibus lutrinis vel murinis thorace 5 confecto umeros ac pectus hieme muniebat, sago veneto

2. 3 obaesa *b*   -que *om. B*   4 hoc *b*   4. 3 assuetus... elixis *om. B*   5. 1 adsidue *Bb*   aequitando *Ab*
23. 1. 1 frantia *b*   2 camisam (*corr. ex* camisiam) *A* ; *cf. Monach. Sangall. p.* 665, *Jaffé,* 18   3 tonicam *b*   4 tum A^2b : tunc *BC* : cum A^1 5 ex *om. b*   lutrinis *om. Bb*
vel murinis *om. BbC*   6 ac pectus] aspectus *b*

amictus et gladio semper accinctus, cuius capulus ac balteus aut aureus aut argenteus erat. Aliquoties et gemmato ense utebatur, quod tamen nonnisi in praecipuis festivitatibus vel si quando exterarum gentium legati venissent. Peregrina vero indumenta, quamvis pulcherrima, respuebat nec umquam eis indui patiebatur, excepto quod Romae semel Hadriano pontifice petente et iterum Leone successore eius supplicante longa tunica et chlamide amictus, calceis quoque Romano more formatis induebatur. In festivitatibus veste auro texta et calciamentis gemmatis et fibula aurea sagum adstringente, diademate quoque ex auro et gemmis ornatus incedebat. Aliis autem diebus habitus eius parum a communi ac plebeio abhorrebat.

24. In cibo et potu temperans, sed in potu temperantior, quippe qui ebrietatem in qualicumque homine, nedum in se ac suis, plurimum abominabatur. Cibo enim non adeo abstinere poterat, ut saepe quereretur noxia corpori suo esse ieiunia. Convivabatur rarissime, et hoc praecipuis tantum festivitatibus, tunc tamen cum magno hominum numero. Cena cotidiana quaternis tantum ferculis praebebatur, praeter assam, quam venatores veribus inferre solebant, qua ille libentius quam ullo alio cibo vescebatur. Inter cenandum aut aliquod acroama aut lectorem audiebat. Legebantur ei historiae et antiquorum res gestae. Delectabatur et libris sancti Augustini, praecipueque his qui *De Civitate Dei* praetitulati sunt. Vini et omnis potus adeo parcus in bibendo erat ut super cenam raro plus quam ter biberet. Aestate post cibum meridianum pomorum aliquid su-

---

2. 1 aliquotiens *B*   3. 3 Adriano *b*   5 chlamide *BC* : clamide *Ab*   **24.** 1. 1 temperatus *b*   2 quacumque *A*   3 abhominabatur *B*   2. 2 incroama *b*   3 res gestae *C* : reges gestae *Bb*[1] : regum gestae *b*[2] : regum gesta *A*   4 Dei] dñi *b*   3. 1 set aestate *B*

mens ac semel bibens, depositis vestibus et calciamentis, velut noctu solitus erat, duabus aut tribus horis quiescebat. Noctibus sic dormiebat ut somnum quater aut quinquies non solum expergiscendo, sed etiam desurgendo interrumperet. Cum calciaretur et amiciretur, non tantum amicos admittebat, verum etiam, si comes palatii litem aliquam esse diceret, quae sine eius iussu definiri non posset, statim litigantes introducere iussit et, velut pro tribunali sederet, lite cognita sententiam dixit ; nec hoc tantum eo tempore, sed etiam quicquid ea die cuiuslibet officii agendum aut cuiquam ministrorum iniungendum erat expediebat.

25. Erat eloquentia copiosus et exuberans poteratque quicquid vellet apertissime exprimere. Nec patrio tantum sermone contentus, etiam peregrinis linguis ediscendis operam impendit : in quibus Latinam ita didicit ut aeque illa ac patria lingua orare sit solitus, Graecam vero melius intellegere quam pronuntiare poterat. Adeo quidem facundus erat ut etiam dicaculus appareret. Artes liberales studiosissime coluit, earumque doctores plurimum veneratus magnis adficiebat honoribus. In discenda grammatica Petrum Pisanum diaconem senem audivit, in ceteris disciplinis Albinum cognomento Alcoinum, item diaconem, de Brittania Saxonici generis hominem, virum undecumque doctissimum, praeceptorem habuit, apud quem et rhetoricae et dialecticae, praecipue tamen astronomiae ediscendae

---

5 sed etiam desurgendo *om. A*   adsurgendo *B*   4. 1 amiciretur *AC* : amictaretur *Bb*   2 amittebat *C*   3 aliquam *ABC et ex corr. b* : aliquem *b*[1]   4 definire *Bb*   6 ne *B*   7 officia *A*   **25.** 1. 7 dicaculus *bC* : didasculus *AB*   2. 2 effitiebat *C*   3 *Fort.* Petrum Pisanum, (Paulum) diaconum; *cf. tamen Poet. Saxon.* v. 233 *sqq. Petrum diaconum audisse testatur Venerius, Duemmler Epp. Kar. Aev. III,* 314, 9   4 diaconem *ABbC*   5 Britania *b* : Brittania *C* : Brittannia *AB*   7 rethoricae *ABbC*

plurimum et temporis et laboris inpertivit. Discebat artem conputandi et intentione sagaci siderum cursum curiosissime rimabatur. Temptabat et scribere tabulasque et codicillos ad hoc in lecto sub cervicalibus circumferre solebat, ut, cum vacuum tempus esset, manum litteris effigiendis adsuesceret, sed parum successit labor praeposterus ac sero inchoatus.

26. Religionem Christianam, qua ab infantia fuerat inbutus, sanctissime et cum summa pietate coluit, ac propter hoc plurimae pulchritudinis basilicam Aquisgrani exstruxit auroque et argento et luminaribus atque ex aere solido cancellis et ianuis adornavit. Ad cuius structuram cum columnas et marmora aliunde habere non posset, Roma atque Ravenna devehenda curavit. Ecclesiam et mane et vespere, item nocturnis horis et sacrificii tempore, quoad eum valitudo permiserat, inpigre frequentabat, curabatque magnopere ut omnia quae in ea gerebantur cum quam maxima fierent honestate, aedituos creberrime commonens ne quid indecens aut sordidum aut inferri aut in ea remanere permitterent. Sacrorum vasorum ex auro et argento vestimentorumque sacerdotalium tantam in ea copiam procuravit, ut in sacrificiis celebrandis ne ianitoribus quidem, qui ultimi ecclesiastici ordinis sunt, privato habitu ministrare necesse fuisset. Legendi atque psallendi disciplinam diligentissime emendavit. Erat enim utriusque admodum eruditus, quamquam ipse nec publice legeret nec nisi submissim et in commune cantaret.

27. Circa pauperes sustentandos et gratuitam liberalitatem, quam Greci eleemosynam vocant, devotissimus,

---

3. 4 codicellos *ABbC* **26.** 2. 3 -que *om. B* 4 quam *C*¹: qua *ABbC*² 8 eam *b* 3. 3 nisi] sibi *A* : sib (*sscr.* ni) *B*
27. 1. 2 eleimosynam *A* : eleimosinam *B* : elemosynam *C* : elymosinam *b, et ita fere ubique* vocant *om. b*

ut qui non in patria solum et in suo regno id facere curaverit, verum trans maria in Syriam et Aegyptum atque Africam, Hierosolimis, Alexandriae atque Kartagini, ubi Christianos in paupertate vivere conpererat, penuriae illorum conpatiens pecuniam mittere solebat, ob hoc maxime transmarinorum regum amicitias expetens, ut Christianis sub eorum dominatu degentibus refrigerium aliquod ac relevatio proveniret.

Colebat prae ceteris sacris et venerabilibus locis apud Romam ecclesiam beati Petri apostoli; in cuius donaria magna vis pecuniae tam in auro quam in argento necnon et gemmis ab illo congesta est. Multa et innumera pontificibus munera missa. Neque ille toto regni sui tempore quicquam duxit antiquius quam ut urbs Roma sua opera suoque labore vetere polleret auctoritate, et ecclesia sancti Petri per illum non solum tuta ac defensa, sed etiam suis opibus prae omnibus ecclesiis esset ornata atque ditata. Quam cum tanti penderet, tamen intra XLVII annorum, quibus regnaverat, spatium quater tantum illo votorum solvendorum ac supplicandi causa profectus est.

28. Ultimi adventus sui non solum hae fuere causae, verum etiam quod Romani Leonem pontificem multis affectum iniuriis, erutis scilicet oculis linguaque amputata, fidem regis implorare conpulerunt. Idcirco Romam veniens propter reparandum, qui nimis conturbatus erat, ecclesiae statum ibi totum hiemis tempus extraxit. Quo tempore Imperatoris et Augusti nomen accepit. Quod primo in tantum aversatus est ut adfirmaret se eo die,

---

3 et] sed *b* 4 siriam *AB* Aegiptum *B* 5 Kartagini *C* Cartagini *b* : Chartagini *A* : Carthagini *B* 7 solebat ret *B* : soleret *b* 10 revelatio *C* (*A*[1] ?) 3. 1 toti *b* 2 antiquus *AC* 3 et *om. B* 4 ecclesiam *Bb* 6 ditata *ABC* : ordinata *b* **28.** 1. 3 adfectum *Bb* 4 regis *om. B* 2. 3 eversatus *B*

quamvis praecipua festivitas esset, ecclesiam non intraturum, si pontificis consilium praescire potuisset. Invidiam tamen suscepti nominis, Romanis imperatoribus super hoc indignantibus, magna tulit patientia. Vicitque eorum contumaciam magnanimitate, qua eis procul dubio longe praestantior erat, mittendo ad eos crebras legationes et in epistolis fratres eos appellando.

29. Post susceptum imperiale nomen, cum adverteret multa legibus populi sui deesse — nam Franci duas habent leges, in plurimis locis valde diversas — cogitavit quae deerant addere et discrepantia unire, prava quoque ac perperam prolata corrigere, sed de his nihil aliud ab eo factum est, nisi quod pauca capitula, et ea inperfecta, legibus addidit. Omnium tamen nationum quae sub eius dominatu erant iura quae scripta non erant describere ac litteris mandari fecit. Item barbara et antiquissima carmina, quibus veterum regum actus et bella canebantur, scripsit memoriaeque mandavit. Inchoavit et grammaticam patrii sermonis.

Mensibus etiam iuxta propriam linguam vocabula inposuit, cum ante id temporis apud Francos partim Latinis, partim barbaris nominibus pronuntiarentur. Item ventos duodecim propriis appellationibus insignivit, cum prius non amplius quam vix quattuor ventorum vocabula possent inveniri. Et de mensibus quidem Ianuarium Wintarmanoth, Februarium Hornung, Martium Lentzinmanoth, Aprilem Ostarmanoth, Maium Winnemanoth, Iunium Brachmanoth, Iulium Heuuimanoth, Augustum Aranmanoth, Septembrem Witumanoth, Octobrem Windumemanoth, Novembrem

---

2. 10 eos fratres *b*   **29.** 1. 3 valde *om. b*   5, 6 ab eo *om. B*
4. 2 uuintarmanot *B*   Febroarium (*ex corr.*) *A*   Hornug *C*
3 Maius *A*   4 iuuinnemanoth *C*   brachmenoth *B*   6 Octubrem *B* : Octembrem *C*   uuindumanoth *B*

Herbistmanoth, Decembrem Heilagmanoth appellavit.
Ventis vero hoc modo nomina inposuit, ut subsolanum
vocaret ostroniwint, eurum ostsundroni, euroaustrum
sundostroni, austrum sundroni, austroafricum sund-
westroni, africum westsundroni, zefyrum westroni,
chorum westnordroni, circium nordwestroni, septen-
trionem nordroni, aquilonem nordostroni, vulturnum
ostnordroni.

30. Extremo vitae tempore, cum iam et morbo et
senectute premeretur, evocatum ad se Hludowicum
filium, Aquitaniae regem, qui solus filiorum Hildigardae
supererat, congregatis sollemniter de toto regno Francorum primoribus, cunctorum consilio consortem sibi
totius regni et imperialis nominis heredem constituit,
inpositoque capiti eius diademate Imperatorem et
Augustum iussit appellari. Susceptum est hoc eius
consilium ab omnibus qui aderant magno cum favore;
nam divinitus ei propter regni utilitatem videbatur
inspiratum. Auxitque maiestatem eius hoc factum et
exteris nationibus non minimum terroris incussit. Di-
misso deinde in Aquitaniam filio, ipse more solito,
quamvis senectute confectus, non longe a regia Aquensi
venatum proficiscitur, exactoque in huiuscemodi negotio
quod reliquum erat autumni, circa Kalendas Novembris
Aquasgrani revertitur.

Cumque ibi hiemaret, mense Ianuario febre valida
correptus decubuit. Qui statim, ut in febribus solebat,
cibi sibi abstinentiam indixit, arbitratus hac continentia

---

7 heribi(e *b*)stmanoth *Bb*   hellagmanoth *B*   5. 1 sola-
num *B*   3 sundostroni austrum *om. B*   sundu uuestroni *b*
4 uust sundroni *A*   westsundroni ... chorum (5) *om. B*
5 nordwestroni *C* : norduuestroni *ABb*   6 nordostroni *Bb*
7 ostnordroni *C* : ostnordroni *ABb*   **30.** 1. 2 et vocatum *b*
Hludoicum *C*   3 Hildegardae *A*   2. 3 ei *om. B*   regni
om. b   4 et *om. b*   10 Aquisgranis *B*   3. 3 in hac *b*

morbum posse depelli vel certe mitigari. Sed accedente
ad febrem lateris dolore, quem Greci pleurisin dicunt,
illoque adhuc inediam retinente neque corpus aliter quam
rarissimo potu sustentante, septimo postquam decubuit
die, sacra communione percepta, decessit, anno aetatis
suae septuagesimo secundo et ex quo regnare coeperat
quadragesimo septimo, V. Kal. Februarii, hora diei tertia.

31. Corpus more sollemni lotum et curatum et maximo
totius populi luctu ecclesiae inlatum atque humatum
est. Dubitatum est primo ubi reponi deberet, eo quod
ipse vivus de hoc nihil praecepisset. Tandem omnium
animis sedit nusquam eum honestius tumulari posse
quam in ea basilica quam ipse propter amorem Dei
et domini nostri Iesu Christi et ob honorem sanctae et
aeternae Virginis, genetricis eius, proprio sumptu in
eodem vico construxit. In hac sepultus est eadem die
qua et defunctus est, arcusque supra tumulum deauratus
cum imagine et titulo exstructus. Titulus ille hoc modo
descriptus est : SVB HOC CONDITORIO SITVM EST
CORPVS KAROLI, MAGNI ATQVE ORTHODOXI
IMPERATORIS, QVI REGNVM FRANCORVM
NOBILITER AMPLIAVIT ET PER ANNOS XLVII
FELICITER REXIT. DECESSIT SEPTVAGENA-
RIVS ANNO DOMINI DCCCXIIII, INDICTIONE
VII, V KAL. FEBR.

32. Adpropinquantis finis conplura fuere prodigia, ut
non solum alii, sed etiam ipse hoc minitari sentiret. Per
tres continuos vitaeque termino proximos annos et solis

---

3. 5 pleuresin *ABbC*   9 et *om. b*   10 Februarii *C* : februa-
rias *ABb*   **31.** 1. 3 debitum *A*   2. 1 est *om. b*   2 qua
et *C* : qua *ABb*   5 ortodoxi *Bb*   7 annos *om. b*   XLVI
codd. Monac. 14641, *Vind.* 969   9 Domini DCCCXIIII
om. BC   indictione *AB* : indicione *b* : indictionis *C*
10 septimo *C* : vi *b* : *om. AB*   **32.** 1. 1 prodigia *BbC* : prae-
sagia *A*

et lunae creberrima defectio et in sole macula quaedam atri coloris septem dierum spatio visa. Porticus, quam inter basilicam et regiam operosa mole construxerat, die ascensionis Domini subita ruina usque ad fundamenta conlapsa. Item pons Rheni apud Mogontiacum, quem ipse per decem annos ingenti labore et opere mirabili de ligno ita construxit ut perenniter durare posse videretur, ita tribus horis fortuitu incendio conflagravit ut, praeter quod aqua tegebatur, ne una quidem hastula ex eo remaneret. Ipse quoque, cum ultimam in Saxoniam expeditionem contra Godofridum regem Danorum ageret, quadam die, cum ante exortum solis castris egressus iter agere coepisset, vidit repente delapsam caelitus cum ingenti lumine facem a dextra in sinistram per serenum aera transcurrere. Cunctisque hoc signum quid portenderet admirantibus, subito equus quem sedebat capite deorsum merso decidit eumque tam graviter ad terram elisit ut, fibula sagi rupta balteoque gladii dissipato, a festinantibus qui aderant ministris exarmatus et sine amiculo levaretur. Iaculum etiam, quod tunc forte manu tenebat, ita elapsum est ut viginti vel eo amplius pedum spatio longe iaceret. Accessit ad hoc creber Aquensis palatii tremor et in domibus ubi conversabatur assiduus laqueariorum crepitus. Tacta etiam de caelo, in qua postea sepultus est, basilica, malumque aureum, quo tecti culmen erat ornatum, ictu fulminis dissipatum et supra domum pontificis, quae basilicae contigua erat, proiectum est. Erat in eadem basilica in margine coronae, quae inter superiores et inferiores arcus interiorem aedis partem ambiebat, epi-

---

2. 2 ipse *om.* b   4 fortuito *C*   5 nec *b*   astula *ABbC*
3. 1 ultima *A*   7 quod *B*   ammirantibus *ABbC*   11 amiculo *C* : amminiculo *ABb*   12 tunc *om. B*   4. 2 quo *B*
3 quod *b*   4 fulminis *C* : fluminis *ABb*

gramma sinopide scriptum, continens, quis auctor esset eiusdem templi, cuius in extremo versu legebatur: KAROLVS PRINCEPS. Notatum est a quibusdam eodem quo decessit anno paucis ante mortem mensibus eas quae PRINCEPS exprimebant litteras ita esse deletas ut penitus non apparerent. Sed superiora omnia sic aut dissimulavit aut sprevit ac si nihil horum ad res suas quolibet modo pertineret.

33. Testamenta facere instituit, quibus filias et ex concubinis liberos ex aliqua parte sibi heredes faceret, sed tarde inchoata perfici non poterant. Divisionem tamen thesaurorum et pecuniae ac vestium aliaeque supellectilis coram amicis et ministris suis annis tribus antequam decederet fecit, contestatus eos ut post obitum suum a se facta distributio per illorum suffragium rata permaneret. Quidque ex his quae diviserat fieri vellet breviario conprehendit; cuius ratio ac textus talis est:

IN NOMINE DOMINI DEI OMNIPOTENTIS, PATRIS ET FILII ET SPIRITVS SANCTI. Descriptio atque divisio, quae facta est a gloriosissimo atque piissimo domno Karolo Imperatore Augusto anno ab incarnatione domini nostri Iesu Christi DCCCºXIº, anno vero regni eius in Francia XLºIIIº et in Italia XXXºVIº, imperii autem XIº, indictione IIIIº, quam pia et prudenti consideratione facere decrevit et Domino annuente perfecit de thesauris suis atque pecunia, quae in illa die in camera eius inventa est. In qua illud praecipue praecavere voluit, ut non solum eleemosynarum largitio, quae sollemniter apud Christianos de possessionibus eorum agitur, pro se quoque de sua pecunia ordine atque ratione perficeretur, sed etiam ut heredes sui omni ambiguitate remota, quid ad se pertinere deberet, liquido cognoscere et sine lite atque

10 notum *B*   est *om. B*   **33.** 1. 10 talis *om. A*

contentione sua inter se conpetenti partitione dividere potuissent.

Hac igitur intentione atque proposito omnem substantiam atque supellectilem suam, quae in auro et argento gemmisque et ornatu regio in illa, ut dictum est, die in camera eius poterat inveniri, primo quidem trina divisione partitus est. Deinde easdem partes subdividendo de duabus partibus XX et unam partem fecit, tertiam integram reservavit. Et duarum quidem partium in XX et unam partem facta divisio tali ratione consistit, ut, quia in regno illius metropolitanae civitates XX et una esse noscuntur, unaquaeque illarum partium ad unamquamque metropolim per manus heredum et amicorum suorum eleemosynae nomine perveniat, et archiepiscopus, qui tunc illius ecclesiae rector exstiterit, partem quae ad suam ecclesiam data est suscipiens cum suis suffraganeis partiatur, eo scilicet modo, ut pars tertia suae sit ecclesiae, duae vero partes inter suffraganeos dividantur. Harum divisionum, quae ex duabus primis partibus factae sunt et iuxta metropoleon civitatum numerum XX et una esse noscuntur, unaquaeque ab altera sequestrata semotim in suo repositorio cum superscriptione civitatis, ad quam perferenda est, recondita iacet. Nomina metropoleon, ad quas eadem eleemosyna sive largitio facienda est, haec sunt: Roma, Ravenna, Mediolanum, Forum Iulii, Gradus, Colonia, Mogontiacus, Iuvavum quae et Salzburg, Treveri, Senones, Vesontio, Lugdunum, Ratumagus, Remi, Arelas, Vienna, Darantasia, Ebrodunum, Burdigala, Turones, Bituriges.

Unius autem partis, quam integram reservari voluit,

---

4. 2 suam *om. b* 9 unam *Bb* 11 nomine *om. b*
13 exstiterit *C* : extiterit *ABb* 5. 1 duobus *A* 2 metropoleon *scripsimus* : metropoleorum *ABbC* 4 cum *om. b*
7 Mediolanium *Ab* 9 Salzburg *A* : Saltzburc *C* : Salzburc *B* : Salzbruch *b* Vesontia *B* Lucdunum *B* 10 Rotumagus *B*
Arelas *AB* : Arales *C* : Areles *b* 11 Burdigula *B*

*talis est ratio ut, illis duabus in supradictas divisiones
distributis et sub sigillo reconditis, haec tertia in usu
cotidiano versaretur, velut res quam nulla voti obligatione
a dominio possidentis alienatam esse constaret, et hoc
tamdiu quoadusque vel ille mansisset in corpore vel usum
eius sibi necessarium iudicaret. Post obitum vero suum
aut voluntariam saecularium rerum carentiam eadem pars
quattuor subdivisionibus secaretur, et una quidem earum
supradictis XX et unae partibus adderetur, altera a filiis
ac filiabus suis filiisque ac filiabus filiorum suorum adsumpta iusta et rationabili inter eos partitione divideretur,
tertia vero consueto Christianis more in usum pauperum
fuisset erogata, quarta simili modo nomine eleemosynae in
servorum et ancillarum usibus palatii famulantium sustentationem distributa veniret. Ad hanc tertiam totius
summae portionem, quae similiter ut ceterae ex auro et
argento constat, adiungi voluit omnia ex aere et ferro
aliisque metallis vasa atque utensilia cum armis et vestibus
alioque aut pretioso aut vili ad varios usus facto supellectili, ut sunt cortinae, stragula, tapetia, filtra, coria,
sagmata, et quicquid in camera atque vestiario eius eo die
fuisset inventum, ut ex hoc maiores illius partis divisiones
fierent et erogatio eleemosynae ad plures pervenire potuisset.
Capellam, id est ecclesiasticum ministerium, tam id quod
ipse fecit atque congregavit, quam quod ad eum ex paterna
hereditate pervenit, ut integrum esset neque ulla divisione
scinderetur ordinavit. Si qua autem invenirentur aut vasa
aut libri aut alia ornamenta, quae liquido constaret eidem
capellae ab eo conlata non fuisse, haec qui habere vellet
dato iustae aestimationis pretio emeret et haberet. Similiter*

6. 4 vel tres *b* 7. 4 adderentur *b* 5 adsumpta] ad supra *b* 7 more] vero *B* 8 quarta vero simili *B*
8. 5 aut] atque *b* aut vilia aut varios *b* 6 sint *Bb*
8 divisionis *A* 9. 5 alia ... eidem *om. B* 6 fuisse *C*: fuisset *ABb*

et de libris, quorum magnam in bibliotheca sua copiam congregavit, statuit, ut ab his qui eos habere vellent iusto pretio fuissent redempti, pretiumque in pauperibus erogatum.

Inter ceteros thesauros atque pecuniam tres mensas argenteas et auream unam praecipuae magnitudinis et ponderis esse constat. De quibus statuit atque decrevit ut una ex his, quae forma quadrangula descriptionem urbis Constantinopolitanae continet, inter cetera donaria quae ad hoc deputata sunt, Romam ad basilicam beati Petri apostoli deferatur, et altera, quae forma rotunda Romanae urbis effigie figurata est, episcopio Ravennatis ecclesiae conferatur. Tertiam, quae ceteris et operis pulchritudine et ponderis gravitate multum excellit, quae ex tribus orbibus conexa totius mundi descriptionem subtili ac minuta figuratione conplectitur, et auream illam, quae quarta esse dicta est, in tertiae illius et inter heredes suos atque in eleemosynam dividendae partis augmento esse constituit.

Hanc constitutionem atque ordinationem coram episcopis, abbatibus comitibusque, qui tunc praesentes esse potuerunt, quorumque hic nomina descripta sunt, fecit atque constituit. *Episcopi:* Hildibaldus, Richolfus, Arn, Wolfarius, Bernoinus, Laidradus, Iohannes, Theodulfus, Iesse, Heito, Waltgaudus. *Abbates:* Fridugisus, Adalungus, Engilbertus, Irmino. *Comites:* Walah, Meginheri, Otulfus, Stephanus, Unruocus, Burchardus, Meginhardus, Hatto, Rihwinus, Edo, Ercangarius, Geroldus, Bero, Hildigernus, Hroccolfus.

10 pauperibus *C*: pauperes *ABb*   10. 7 et ... conferatur *om. B*   8 effigiae *Ab*   12 esse *om. b*   14 augmentum *Bb*
11. 4 Hildebaldus *AB*: Hildeboldus *b*: Hildi(*ex* e *corr.*)bald *C*   Arn *om. C*   Vuolpharius *C*   Bernoin *A*   5 Laidrad *Bb*   Theodolfus *C*: Theotulfus *B*   Hetto *b*   6 uualdgaudus *b*   Fridigisus *Bb*   Adalunc *b*   Engilberdus *A*   7 walah *Ab*: uualath *C*: uualag *B*   Otolfus *C*   8 Buruchardus *b*   Meginhartus *b*   Atto *B*   9 Rihuuinnus *B*: Richuuinus *b*   Erchangarius *b*   Hildigernus *C*: Hildegernus *B*: Hildigern *A*: Hiltigern *b*

12   Haec omnia filius eius Hludowicus, qui ei divina iussione successit, inspecto eodem breviario, quam celerrime poterat post obitum eius summa devotione adimplere curavit.

EXPLICIT

12. 1 Haec ... curavit *om. C*   Hludoicus *B*   divina ei *b*
4 *Post* curavit *add.* EXPLICIT *b*   *Sequuntur in Bb versus Gerwardi : vide Introd. p. viii.*

NOTES

WALAHFRIDI PROLOGUS

Walafrid Strabo (or Strabus) was a pupil of Rabanus Maurus, and so a 'grand-pupil' of Alcuin. Like Einhard, he was educated at Fulda. He became tutor to Charles the Bald, and abbot of Reichenau in Switzerland. He must have edited Einhard's *Life of Charlemagne* not long after the death of its author, since he died himself in the year 849.

1 *quae subiecta sunt*, 'which follow'; a phrase from legal Latin.

palatinos, 'members of the palace school' of Charlemagne.

laudis egregiae: with *vir* (2), 'a man of outstanding eminence'.

2 *Natus* e.q.s. See Introd., p. xiii.

Bonifacii. Fulda was founded in 744 by S. Sturm, under the direction of Boniface; see *Vita S. Sturmi*, pp. 367–8, Pertz.

avidissimus with *inquirere*, 'most eager to search out'.

excolere: not 'to frequent their society', but 'to furnish them with all that they required'.

ideo . . . reddidit, 'and so he illumined with a light of universal science, new, and in part undreamed of by our barbarous age, the cloudy (and, in a figure, visionless) length and breadth of the kingdom which God had entrusted to his care'.

relabentibus in contraria studiis. The complaint is exaggerated. There were still great lights of learning —Servatus Lupus, Sedulius, Iohannes Scottus, Heiricus, Ermenricus, Paschasius Radbertus, to say nothing of Walafrid's own teacher Rabanus.

3 *Praedictus itaque homuncio*, i.e. Einhard. *praedictus, antedictus, supradictus, praefatus, antefatus, praenominatus, memoratus*, etc., 'the afore-mentioned' are favourite-resumptive formulae in mediaeval Latin (see e.g. *Vit. Kar.* ii. 3) and illustrate the influence of legal Latin upon the mediaeval diction. For *homuncio* see Introd., p. xv.

merito, ' by reason of '.

nullus = nemo, as xx. 2 *ullus = quisquam*.

mira ... libratione, ' a marvellous adjustment of behaviour over which Providence itself seemed to watch '.

ipsum ... manciparit, ' neither abandoned our hero unseasonably nor delivered him over to irremediable disasters '. *manciparit*: another trace of legal Latin; the word is so used several times in the *Codex Theodosianus*, and recurs in *Vita Kar.* at xviii. 5.

4 *dum non ignoret*, ' in so far as he is not ignorant ', i. e., seeing that he will have good assurance.

provectoris sui, ' the author of his advancement ', sc. Charlemagne.

debere, ' feels the obligation ', not merely to deliver a panegyric of his master, but also to tell the truth to the serious inquirer. *curiositati* means not ' curiosity ', but the spirit of careful historical research, the Greek ἱστορία.

titulos et incisiones, ' headings and chapters '. Walafrid divided the work into thirty-nine chapters. His *tituli* may be seen in the edition of Waitz-Holder-Egger.

ut ad singula ... accessus, ' in order that the reader when looking up some point which has attracted his attention may have the readier and more obvious (*elucescat*) access to it '.

quod placuerit, ' which he has determined to find '.

EINHARDI PROLOGUS

TITULUS. *dictata*, ' composed '—a very common use of the word in mediaeval Latin. It has its origin in the once common practice of dictating compositions to a professional scribe (*scriba, antiquarius, notarius*). It is mostly used only of composition in prose, but sometimes also of poetic composition (Wattenbach, *Schriftwesen*, pp. 457–61).

1 *Vitam ... conplexus sum*, ' Having resolved to write an account of the life and habits, and, in some measure, of the achievements of a great and justly famous king, my lord and foster-father Charles, I have endeavoured to make my narrative as brief as possible '.

nova quaeque fastidientium, ' readers who are contemptuous of anything modern ',

si tamen ... offendantur, ' though I fear it is almost impossible to avoid offending, in a modern composition '.

NOTES

2 *Et quamquam*, ' And, though I do not doubt that there are many lovers of learned leisure who do not so utterly despise the modern world as to think that all contemporary history should be left to silence and oblivion, as a record not worth keeping, but who would prefer, allured by the hope of an abiding fame, to make even poor literature out of the great deeds of others rather than, by writing nothing, to deprive posterity of the fame of their own eminence; yet even so I have not felt it my duty to desist from the kind of work which I here offer '.

oculata . . . fide, ' the testimony of my own eyes '. Plautus uses the phrase *oculatus testis* (opposed to *auritus testis*); but *oculata fide* has come to Einhard from such sources as *Instit. Iustin.* iii. 6. 9. The phrase is found also in *Dial. de Scaccario*, iv, ch. vii, Stubbs, *Charters*.

et utrum . . . non potui, ' and had no means of knowing clearly (*liquido*) whether any one else had undertaken to record them '. The different mediaeval centres of learning (the monasteries) tended to be a good deal isolated. Traube has pointed out that of many excellent works of mediaeval literature the repute never went further than the monastery in which each was composed (*Einl. in d. lat. Phil. d. M.*, p. 36).

moderni: a word formed (on the analogy of *hodiernus*) from *modo*, the mediaeval equivalent for the classical *nunc*.

3 *nutrimentum . . . inpensum*, ' the fostering care lavished upon me ', including not merely material, but spiritual, benefits.

4 *Cui scribendae . . . facundiam*, ' to record and illustrate which were a labour worthy, not of my poor abilities—for they are slender, dwarfish, nay, non-existent—but even of the eloquence of Cicero '. *cui scribendae* and *desudare* (to *sweat over*, toil at) go together; in classical Latin we should have *in qua scribenda*.

barbarus, ' German '; as chap. xxix *barbara carmina, barbaris nominibus*. Bede applies *barbara loquela* to the Frankish speech, in contrast to Anglo-Saxon.

Tusculanarum, sub. *Disputationum*. The reference is to *Tusc. Disp.* i. 3. 6. The careful study of Cicero is evident throughout the *Vita*. Besides the *Tusc. Disp.* Einhard had evidently studied carefully the Speech for Milo, and the Speeches against Verres and Catiline.

EINHARDI VITA KAROLI

CHAPTER I

1 *Hildrichum.* Childeric III, who reigned from 743–51.

Stephani. Stephen III (sometimes reckoned, more correctly, as Stephen II). Einhard's account is not strictly accurate. It was Pope Zacharias who allowed (he did not ' bid ') Pepin the Short to depose Childeric. (Zacharias wanted the aid of Pepin against the Lombards, and against Byzantium.) It was Pope Stephen, however, who crowned Pepin at St. Denys in 754. The same error appears in the *Chronographia* of Theophanes, ed. Bonn. 619; and again in the *Breviarium* of Erchambert, Pertz, p. 328.

monasterium. The St. Bertin *Annals* specify *in Sithiu monasterium* (in north-west Flanders), and so here (transferred thence), one of our MSS. The Lobbes *Annals* say *in monasterio S. Medardi est attonsus* (in both cases against the year 750).

The Cloister was the prison-house of a good many dispossessed princes of the Merovingian and Carolingian houses : in the sixth century Hlodoald (St. Cloud), son of Hlodimir, son of Clovis, and Merovech, son of Chilperic I ; in the seventh, Theuderich the father, and Dagobert the son, of Sigebert II ; in the eighth Carloman, son of Charles Martel, together with his sons (747 ; said to be a voluntary retirement : see chap. ii) ; Childeric III (here mentioned, 752) ; the sons of Carloman, brother of Charlemagne (774) ; Pepin the Hunchback, son of Charlemagne (792).

2 *palatii praefectos*: one of the many names by which the ' Mayors of the Palace ' are spoken of. Others are *palatii praepositi, custodes, gubernatores, magistri : aulae praefecti, maiores domus.* All these phrases probably render an original O.G. *Meier*, a ' steward '. We hear of ' mayors ' under the earliest Merovingian kings, e. g. Clovis' son, Lothair I. The early mayors seem to have had little political importance, and to have been appointed by the king. They were bailiffs of the royal estates. The mayor as a political and military official, controlling king and kingdom, seems to be the creation of the Austrasians. He was appointed by the chiefs to act as a check on the kingly power. The office became a life-office under Lothair II. The institution is bor-

NOTES: CHAPTER I. 1-3

rowed from Austrasia by the Neustrians and Burgundians: but in Neustria the mayor appears rather as the protector of the king in his struggles with the chiefs than as representing the interests of the latter. The office first became 'officium velut hereditarium' (chap. ii, *init.*) with Pepin of Landen, great-grandfather to Charles Martel. Grimoald, son of Pepin of Landen, tried unsuccessfully to anticipate the revolution carried through by Pepin, son of Charles Martel—to consign the Merovingian king to a monastery and to seize for himself the vacant throne.

crine profuso, barba summissa. The long hair and beard are a symbol rather of priestly than of kingly functions. The Merovingians are priest-kings: their sacred persons would have been profaned by the steel instruments of the barber. This taboo dates back to a period in Frankish history prior to the steel, or iron, age. A similar taboo is found in the ancient Roman priesthood (Davis, p. 28).

See Agathias, p. 14, A, 524 θεμιτὸν γὰρ τοῖς βασιλεῦσι τῶν Φράγκων οὐ πώποτε κείρεσθαι : Theophanes, i. 6. 19 (cited by Freeman, *Western Europe in the VIIIth Century*, p. 26) ἐλέγοντο δ' ἐκ τοῦ γένους ἐκείνου καταγόμενοι κριστάται, ὃ ἑρμηνεύεται τριχοραχάται· τρίχας γὰρ εἶχον κατὰ τῆς ῥάχης ἐκφυομένας, ὡς χοῖροι : Erchambert, p. 328, Pertz, 'Merovei . . sicut antiquitus Nazaraei, nullo capitis crine inciso erant.'

precarium vitae stipendium : not 'the precarious boon of life' (as Davis, p. 28), but 'an uncertain pittance wherewith to sustain life'—as appears from the qualifying clause *quod . . . exhibebat.*

praeparvi reditus villam, 'a country estate bringing in but a small revenue'. The use of *prae, per* as intensive prefixes of adjectives is characteristic of mediaeval usage. Classical Latin would require here *perparvi* (*prae* conveying the notion of advantage).

in qua . . . ex qua. The distinction is that between the *terra indominicata*, the property immediately surrounding the royal residence, and the *mansi*, or small holdings, tilled by dependent cultivators under conditions of dues, &c. (See Vinogradoff, *Cambridge Mediaeval History*, ii, pp. 649-50.) Childeric's residence was at Montmacq.

numerositatis: frequent in both legal and biblical Latin.

3 *carpento.* This again was obligatory on the king, as priest. Einhard wrongly regards it as imposed upon him by the mayor as an indignity. For the *carpentum* as a ceremonial vehicle see Isidore, *Etym.* xx. 12. 3

'carpentum pompaticum vehiculi genus [est], quasi carrum pompaticum'.

conventum : the Marchfield or (later, after 755) Mayfield (*campus Martius, campus Madius*); the great annual assembly of king, nobles, and commons, held in March or (later) May.

annuatim. These adverbs in *-im* are characteristic of mediaeval Latin; cf. xxii *perpetim*, xxvi *submissim*, xxxiii *semotim.* On the analogy of *annuatim* we get also *diatim*.

CHAPTER II

2 *Karolus.* Charles Martel, 'the Hammer', Karolus Tudetes.

tyrannos. Einhard speaks somewhat vaguely. He probably refers to (1) Chilperic II (715–20), and his mayor Raganfred; (2) Maurontus, Duke of Provence; as well as (3) Odo, Duke of Aquitaine. Chilperic, defeated at Amblève (716), Viney (717), took refuge with Odo from the pursuit of Charles; but Odo surrendered him (719–20). Subsequently, however, Odo allied himself with the Saracens against Charles, and suffered defeat (732), *Chron. Moiss.*, p. 291, Pertz. Maurontus also entered into an alliance with the Saracens, with like fortune (738–9). See *Ann. Lauriss. Min.*, a. 715–41, pp. 114–15, Pertz; and *Ann. Lauresh.* and *Alemann.*, p. 24 : cf. *Ann. Petau* and *Tilian.*

Pictavium : Poitiers.

Birram fluvium : about seven miles from Narbonne (737).

a populo. Of a *popular* election of the mayors there is no evidence in any period. See on chap. i. 2.

eundem magistratum : the office of mayor of the palace.

3 *Hunc* : sc. *magistratum*.

velut sub rege memorato, ' as though under the direction (under the nominal direction) of the king I have mentioned ', *sc.* Childeric III.

Soracte : Monte S. Oreste in Tuscany. (S. Oreste appears to be merely a vulgar corruption of the name Soracte.)

4 *Samnium* : the Abruzzi.

castro Casino. The monastery of Monte Cassino, founded by St. Benedict in 529, remained throughout the Middle Ages a principal centre of European culture.

Chapter III

1 *per annos XV.* It should be XVI (752–68).

Waifarium. Pepin invaded Aquitania in 760—' cernens Waifarium, ducem Aquitaniorum, minime consentire iustitias ecclesiarum partibus quae erant in Francia' (*Ann. Lauriss.* a. 760; cf. *Ann. Mettens.*, p. 333, Pertz). But the quarrel between the two was an old one. In particular Waifer had lent his countenance, twelve years earlier, to Grifo, Pepin's half-brother, whom the partial historians describe as 'rebelling' (741) against Pepin and Carloman, and who in 747 escaped from the prison to which his brothers had consigned him and fled into Aquitaine (*Ann. Lauriss.* a. 748). Waifer in 760 gave oaths and hostages, but immediately went back upon both. The war dragged on for nine years, interrupted by Pepin's Bavarian War (764–5). It ended with the death of Waifer in 768. Pepin himself died on September 24 of the same year. In the following year Aquitaine again broke into rebellion (chap. v, *init.*).

morbo aquae intercutis: the dropsy.

2 *siquidem,* 'indeed'; a frequent mediaeval usage, employed several times in this book.

reges constituunt. They had already been crowned, together with their father, by Pope Stephen, in 754; and in 768 Pepin had himself divided his kingdom between them. They were, however, consecrated again on October 9, 768, and, perhaps, then ratified anew the partition of the kingdom made by their father. (See the continuation of the *Chronicle of Fredegar*, pp. 192–3, Kursch, and *Ann. Mettens.*, p. 335, Pertz.)

ex aequo partirentur. To Charlemagne fell Austrasia and most of Neustria, to Carloman Burgundy, Provence, South-east Aquitaine, and Alemannia.

quam ... Pippinus ... cui ... Karlomannus. Einhard would seem to be in error here. Charles Martel had assigned to Pepin Austrasia, Alemannia, Thuringia: and to Carloman Neustria, Burgundy, and Provence. (So the continuation of *Fredegar's Chronicle* (p. 179, Kursch), *Chron. Moissiac.* (p. 292, Pertz), and *Ann. Mettens.* a. 741, p. 327, Pertz.)

regendi gratia, 'to rule over' (with *susciperet*). This use of *gratia* is characteristic of the period; cf. e. g. *Ann. Einh.* a. 786 'obsidatus gratia': it comes from the legal Latin.

3 *Mansitque ... concordia.* See chap. xviii, *init.*, and Introd., pp. xviii sqq.

multis ex parte Karlomanni. This may or may not be

true. But there would seem to have been at the court of Carloman a considerable faction of friends of Charlemagne. This faction was, perhaps, largely ecclesiastical—led by Wilcharius and Folradus (see *Ann. Lauriss.* a. 771). It is significant that Charlemagne's plans were fully matured when his brother died—there is no hesitation in the action which he takes (771). On the so-called reconciliation between the two brothers in the year 770 see Introd., p. xx.

uxor. One of our MSS. here calls her Teoberga. Her name was probably Gerberga. She is called Berterad by Andreas (p. 224, Waitz), and in the Lobbes *Annals*, p. 228, is said to have been a daughter of Didier, King of the Lombards. This is a confusion—the name of the daughter of Didier whom Charlemagne married is also given as Berterad (see below); and it is quite certain from Cod. Carol. Ep. 47, Jaffé, that Carloman married a Frankish wife. Gerberga had two infant sons. Both the mother and the children fell into Charlemagne's hands when he took Verona in 774. They were never heard of again, and the historian is left to infer from his general preconceptions of Charlemagne's character whether he consigned them to some religious prison-house or to the grave. Of this Einhard discreetly says nothing. On the attitude of Didier towards the two children see below, vi. 1.

quibusdam. Chief among these faithful few was Ogier (Otger, Autchaire) the Dane, who ended his life in the monastery of St. Faro. See *Lib. Pont.*, Duchesne, pp. 487–8, 493, 495–6.

Desiderii. Didier. Charlemagne married, and almost immediately divorced in the most heartless way, this king's daughter. Einhard never tells us her name—perhaps he had forgotten it, just as he tells us in chap. xix that he has forgotten that of one of Charlemagne's concubines (who, however, were even more numerous than his wives). It is usually given as Desiderata (Désirée) (*Vita Adelhardi*, p. 235, Pertz); wrongly according to Hellmann, *Neues Archiv*, xxxiv, pp. 208 sqq. But see also Abel, *Jahrb. Karl des Grossen*, p. 66. Andreas gives her name as Berterad (Bertha), p. 223, Waitz; and he also states (we shall hardly believe him), that Charlemagne divorced her to please Carloman. Other authorities (e.g. the *Monk of S. Gall*) assign for the divorce the same reasons as those which led Napoleon to divorce Josephine.

4 *biennio.* It should be *triennio.* The *Ann. Lauriss.* have correctly 'tres annos' (October 768–December 771).

Chapter IV

1 *nativitate.* It has been conjectured, without much plausibility, that Einhard had good reasons for 'knowing nothing' about the birth of Charlemagne. According to the S. Bertin *Annals* the marriage of his father Pepin with Bertha (Bertrada) was not solemnized until 750. (This date is perhaps inferred from the Petau *Annals* (p. 11, Pertz), the author of which places the birth of *Carloman* in 751.) Charlemagne certainly died in 814 (January 28). At chap. xxx, *fin.* Einhard tells us that he was then in his seventy-second year. But in his epitaph (chap. xxxi, *fin.*), he is spoken of as *septuagenarius*. The epitaph is naturally our safest guide. But it is a question whether *septuagenarius* may not there mean merely 'a man in his seventh decade'—perhaps with a vague reference to the years allowed to man by the Psalmist. On the other hand, *septuagesimo secundo* in chap. xxx (which re-appears, however, in *Not. Sangall. Hist.*, Pertz, p. 71) [1] may very well be a copyist's blunder—LXXII for LXXI; and this solution would reconcile the date in this chapter, not only with *septuagenarius*, but also with *Ann. Lauriss.* a. 814, *init.* (*septuagesimo primo*) [2]—a part of the *Ann. Lauriss.* which is supposed to proceed from Einhard. The birth of Charlemagne would thus fall in the year 743.

It is possible that *nativitate* means here merely 'horoscope'.

2 *narrando* : with both *res gestas* and *de administratione.*

Chapter V

1 *auxilium ferre rogato.* Charlemagne and Carloman, in the division of their father's kingdom each took a part of Aquitaine. It was natural, therefore, that they should co-operate in crushing this rising. It is to be noted that Einhard does not say, as our histories do, that Carloman refused to assist his brother. The words *promisso frustrasset auxilio* below show clearly that the charge against Carloman was that, *after promising assistance*, he had failed to give it—a very different thing, since the trouble in Aquitaine proved only a somewhat trivial affair, and it is possible that what really occurred was that Carloman's aid came too late.

---

[1] But there against the year 715. Thegan's *Life of Louis* also has LXXII (p. 592, Pertz).

[2] So too the Würzburg *Annals*, a. 814.

In any case it cannot have been badly needed. It is also worth remarking that the first part of the Fulda *Annals* and the *Ann. Lauriss. Minores* represent the conquest of Aquitaine as the joint work of the two brothers (pp. 348 and 117, Pertz).

iugitate, 'prolonged effort'. As = 'duration', it occurs in *Cod. Iustin.* i. 7. 5.

2   *Hunoldum*: Hunald[1] the father of Waifer, defeated by Pepin and Carloman in 742, had retired to a monastery in the Île de Rhé. The *Ann. Lauriss.* a. 769 identify this Hunald with the person mentioned in this chapter, supposing him, apparently, to have emerged from his monastery on the death of Waifer, and to have raised rebellion in Aquitaine. On the other hand, the reviser of the *Ann. Lauriss.*, sometimes identified with Einhard, speaks of the Hunald of this chapter as *Hunoldus quidam*, deliberately correcting, as it would seem, the *Ann. Lauriss.* Most writers seem now content to regard this Hunald as some pretender who bore, or assumed, the name of Waifer's father. Lavisse states that Waifer's father had been dead for thirteen years, but he cites no authority for the statement (*Hist. de France*, ii. 1. 281). It is unlikely that Waifer's father would have taken refuge with Loup (Lupus), Duke of Gascony, as did our Hunald. For the old Hunald had treated the family of Loup in such a way that he was likely to meet (as, indeed, did our Hunald) with scant mercy.

transmisso amne Garonna. Some MSS. add (doubtless from the *Ann. Lauriss.* q. v.) *et aedificato castro Frontiaco*, in allusion to the fortress of Fronsac, which Charlemagne built to command the passage of the Dordogne, an important strategical point.

Chapter VI

1   *Hadriani*: Adrian I succeeded Stephen III in 772.

exoratus: Einhard's account of this matter is strangely wanting in frankness. Gerberga, the widow of Carloman, had, with her two children, taken refuge wth Didier, (Desiderius), King of the Lombards (chap. iii, *fin.*). Didier, already deeply wronged by Charlemagne, who had divorced his daughter, undertook to restore these children to the throne of their father. With this purpose he desired Pope Adrian to crown them. This Adrian refused to do; and

[1] He was the son of the Duke Odo, who had defied Charles Martel in 720   See on ii. **2**.

Didier, levying war, actually laid siege to Rome. The Pope then appealed to Charlemagne, who, after a good deal of diplomatic delay (his soldiers probably liked this Italian adventure as little as did those of Pepin), marched two armies into Lombardy.

The quarrel, therefore, was as much Charlemagne's as the Pope's, and its origin was not particularly creditable to Charles. It is true, however, that there were deeper causes of hostility between the Papacy and the Lombard kingdom than the refusal of Adrian to crown the sons of Carloman. That portion of the old Imperial territory known as the Exarchate cut in two the territories of the Lombards. It had been won for the Lombard kingdom by Didier's predecessor, Aistulf (Adolphus). In 754 Pope Stephen had invoked the assistance of Pepin, the father of Charlemagne, and Pepin, after defeating Aistulf at Pavia (Ticino), had bestowed upon the Papacy the disputed territories. These lands Didier no doubt plotted now to recover, and Charlemagne's cause acquired an honourable appearance when he could pose as the vindicator of the so-called 'Donation of Pepin'.

2   *paucorum dierum obsidione.* This is very inexact. Pepin twice invaded Italy and attacked Aistulf, first in 754, and then in 756. Einhard apparently knows nothing of the invasion of 754.

Italia excedere: Adalghis took refuge at the Byzantine court, where his presence furnished a welcome excuse for Eastern intrigue in the West.

Hruodgausum Foroiuliani ducatus praefectum. Two years after Charlemagne had overthrown the Lombard kingdom, he discovered that his work was not finished. He had left most of the Lombard dukes in possession of their duchies, as his dependents (*praefecti*). Of these one of the most powerful was Rotgaud, duke of Friuli (Forum Iulii, in the Venetian territory). Charlemagne was still involved in the first of his Saxon wars, when Rotgaud raised the standard of rebellion. Rotgaud was defeated and killed in the first encounter, and his cause quickly collapsed.

Pippinum regem inponeret. This was not until seven years later (781).

4   *perpetuo exilio deportatus.* See *Ann. Sangall. Mai.*, p. 75, Pertz 'Rex Desiderius et Ansa uxor eius pariter exiliati sunt (ad Corbeiam, et ibi Desiderius in vigiliis et orationibus et ieiuniis et multis bonis operibus permansit usque ad diem obitus sui)'. The *Ann. Lauriss. Min.* include Desiderius' daughter in this exile; the Lobbes *Annals* more than one daughter, cf. *n.* on xi. 1.

Chapter VII

1 *quasi intermissum videbatur*, 'which was regarded as having merely been dropped for a while'. The intermission referred to is that caused by the campaign against Didier (773–4), and not the second break, caused by the rebellion of Rotgaud and the Lombard dukes in 776 (though Einhard has already, in passing, dealt with this rebellion). The Saxon Wars lasted from 772–804. We may distinguish three main periods : (1) 772–9, consisting of four campaigns, of which the last was connected with the revolt of Witikin. In 779 Saxony was divided into administrative districts for the dissemination of the Christian religion ; (2) 782–5 : the trouble began with a new rising by Witikin, distinguished by the expulsion and slaughter of Charlemagne's missionaries. The principal event of it was the Battle of Detmold, mentioned below by Einhard. In 785 Christianity was enforced by a death-penalty, and Witikin himself submitted to baptism ; (3) 793–804 : the submission of Witikin had virtually ended the Saxon resistance : but during the twelve years 793–804 there were intermittent outbreaks—the principal fighting took place in the years 794–6.

Saxon and Frank had been at war as early as the sixth century. Lothair I had made the Saxons pay tribute. But throughout the eighth century there had been constant Saxon raids into Frankish territory. Charles Martel and Pepin the Short had kept the Saxons in tolerable subjection. But they were still a military peril—and they were heathen. Charlemagne opened the campaign of 772 by a blow which in itself sufficiently reveals his motives —the destruction of the sacred Irminsul, the world-sustaining Pillar ('universalis columna, quasi sustinens omnia').

The Saxons occupied at this period roughly the whole of Northern Germany from the Rhine to the Elbe.

nostrae religioni contrarii. Einhard seizes rightly the essential characteristic of the Saxon Wars. They are religious crusades. The penalty of defeat is baptism. Charlemagne, throughout his dealings with the Saxons, shrank from no extreme of cruelty which might move an untutored people to accept the gospel of mercy. See Anon. *Vita Ludov.* chap. i 'ad agnitionem confessionemque veritatis *quoquo modo* perduceret'.

2 *suberant et causae*, 'there were other subordinate causes' —but the main cause was not political but religious.

in plano contigui, 'contiguous in regions offering no

NOTES: CHAPTERS VII. 1—IX

natural barriers' (of mountain, &c.), *in plano* qualified by the parenthesis *praeter . . . disterminant*.

vicissitudinem reddere, ' to make reprisals '.

3 *absque* = *sine*: a constant mark of the mediaeval period.

5 *decem milia*: an understatement. In 797 alone Charles removed a third of the Saxon population, in addition to 7,000 transported in 794; and there were other large evictions in other years. It is to be noted that Einhard says not a word of the massacre of Verden; see Introd., p. xxv.

Albis: the Elbe.

6 *adunati*: a Biblical and patristic word, perhaps employed here intentionally, to sort with ' *unus populus* ', etc. But perhaps a blunder of the MSS. for *adiuncti* (the same confusion occurs in Cic. *Off*. iii. 8. 35).

CHAPTER VIII

1 *Osneggi*: Mt. Osning.

Theotmelli: Detmold. The battle took place in the summer of 783, when the Westphalians were utterly defeated.

Hasam fluvium: the Haase, a tributary of the Ems. The battle took place at Schlachtverderberg (now ' die Elus '), near Osnabrück, against the Angrarii, in the same summer.

2 *contra Francos exorta*: Einhard is always careful to represent Charlemagne's wars as *forced upon him*; cf. xiii. **3** ' bellum contra Francos exortum ', and xiii. **5**.

3 *biennio ante Italicum, etc.*, ' the war began two years before the Italian war '; before the war against Didier, that is.

sine intermissione. It is spoken of in vii, *init*. as ' *quasi* intermissum '.

falso blandienti fortunae adsentiri, ' to be wheedled by the delusive flattery of success ' (*falso*, adv.).

CHAPTER IX

It is to be observed that in this chapter Einhard tells us nothing either of the causes or the results of Charlemagne's incursions into Spain. Later historians assign a religious motive ('laboranti ecclesiae sub Saracenorum acerbissimo iugo Christo fautore suffragari ', Anon. *Vita Lud*. 2), and represent the expedition as sent to aid the Christians against the Saracens. Yet the first town which Charlemagne took was the Christian town of Pampeluna. Spain was at this time under the rule of the Saracen Abderrahman. The very name of the Saracen was odious in Christian ears, but Abderrahman seems to have governed Spain moderately and competently. It was not the Spanish Christians who invited Charlemagne's interference in Spain, but a small faction of malcontent Saracens who had a dynastic quarrel with Abderrahman. Einhard would be as anxious to cover up this alliance between his master and the Saracen plotters, as he is to conceal the general futility of the expedition, which had no result at all at the time ; it was not until 795 that Charlemagne's generals added to the Frankish kingdom the region known as the Spanish March.—The *Ann. Lauriss.* omit all mention of the Roncesvalles disaster.

1 *quam maximo poterat*, ' as large as he could manage ' ; cf. chap. xxvi ' cum quam maxima . . . honestate'.

in ipso Pyrinei iugo: not Roncesvalles, but an older pass to the west, though the defeat has become inseparably associated with the name of Roncesvalles.

parumper . . . experiri, ' to make a momentary trial of '.

2 *agmine longo . . . porrectus*, ' in a long straggling column '.

eos qui . . . tuebantur, ' those who, marching at the tail of the column, served as an armed escort to the train in front of them '. *novissimi*, nom. pl., *incedentes*, nom. pl., *praecedentes*, acc. pl. *praecedentes* is, therefore, the baggage-train, whose rear was protected by soldiery. *subsidio* with *tuebantur*.

subiectam vallem, ' the valley beneath '.

3 *iniquitas*, ' the uneven character of the ground '.

per omnia, ' in all respects '—with *impares*.

regiae mensae praepositus, ' the royal Seneschal '.

comes palatii, ' count of the palace ', ' Paladin '.

Hruodlandus Brittannici limitis praefectus, ' Roland, the Warden of the Breton March '.

A whole family of MSS. omit this clause. Yet it appears in the oldest MS. of all, *A*, which was written before 850. It is difficult to believe that any form of the Roland legend had at a date so early as this so strongly established itself as to offer temptation to an interpolator—we could easily believe this if our MSS. were a century later. It seems on the whole best to suppose a merely accidental omission in the parent MS. of the *B* family (the individual MSS. of this family are characterized by endless such accidental omissions). The clause was perhaps not known to the ' Saxon Poet ' who has versified Einhard's *Life* for us (*Poeta Saxo*, i. 390–91). It must also be admitted that there is no very good reason why Roland should have been with the baggage train ; whereas the ' comes palatii ' and the ' regiae mensae praepositus ' have their place there (a point seized by the *Poeta Saxo*).

ad praesens: the disaster took place on August 15, 778.

Chapter X

1 *domuit et Brittones*. This is an overstatement, and the more so if it is taken solely in connexion with the expedition mentioned in line 3. That expedition was entrusted to the *praepositus regiae mensae* Audulfus, in 786. But in 799 a new expedition was necessary; and, although in 800 the Breton chiefs made a general submission to Charlemagne, there were renewed troubles shortly before Charlemagne's death. Brittany owed its independent spirit to the new blood which had been infused into the old Gallo-Roman population by the settlement in the Armorican peninsula, in the sixth century, of the Celts who fled from England under stress of the Anglo-Saxon invasion.

2 *Italiam ingressus*: in the winter of 786–7.

Aragisus. Areghis, Duke of Benevento, had been distantly implicated in the rebellion of Rotgaud, already mentioned; see on vi. 2: and in 781 he had leagued himself with the Patrician of Sicily, and possibly with Tassilo, Duke of Bavaria, in a desultory warfare against the Pope. But in 786 he assumed the style and title of an independent king, with promise of support both from Constantinople and from the Bavarians.

imperata . . . cogeretur, 'undertook to obey any order short of being compelled to appear in person before Charlemagne'.

3 *utilitate gentis*, 'the interests of the Lombards'.

pro magno munere: not 'in return for a considerable present', but 'as a great privilege'.

qui minor erat: Grimoldus: *maiorem* = Rumoldum.

Romam redit. At the Papal court he met the envoys of Tassilo, who, owing to the influence of the Pope, was compelled to make his submission to Charlemagne, though not until he had actually encountered Charlemagne's armies (xi. 2 sqq.).

Chapter XI

1 *Baioaricum*: Bavarian.

uxoris. Her name was Liutberga. As the sister of Desiderius, she had been the sister-in-law of Charlemagne.

patris. The not very reliable Andreas says that Desiderius died in 774. We know nothing of his fate save what Einhard tells us at vi, *fin.*, which is consistent with this passage and inconsistent with Andreas. It seems none the less possible that *patris* here is a blunder for *fratris*; see

Crit. Note. Liutberga's brother was Adalghis, at this time a scheming exile in Byzantium (see on vi. 2), and an essential part (as the father could hardly have been) of the present plot.

Hunis. It should be *Avaribus* ; but the historians of the period failed to distinguish the two peoples : see xiii. 1 'Avares vel Hunos', Alcuin, *Epp.* 7, p. 32, Duemmler, 'Avari quos nos Hunos dicimus'. Tassilo's pact with the Avars was betrayed to Charlemagne by Tassilo's own men (' fideles Baioarii ', *Ann. Lauriss.*).

2 *Lechum amnem* : the Lech, a river which falls into the Danube near Ingolstadt. *Ann. Lauriss.* specify ' in loco ubi Lechfeld vocatur '.

3 *genti utile.* Tassilo's army would not fight—they had been alarmed by a Papal anathema.

4 *finis impositus.* A good deal is suppressed here ; and the order of events is confused. A clearer account may be found in the *Ann. Lauriss.* The conspiracy of Tassilo with the Avars is subsequent to the submission which followed the encounter by the River Lech. This submission took place in 787. It was in 788 that Tassilo invoked the aid of the Avars, and was finally crushed by Charlemagne. He was condemned to death, but subsequently permitted by Charlemague to retire to the monastery of Jumièges. The settlement of Bavaria briefly noticed in the last sentence of the chapter dates from 788. The clemency by which Charlemagne spared the life of Tassilo has been interpreted as evidence of an uneasy conscience. The guilt of Tassilo is assumed by Einhard without question. But it seems to have been questioned by others, even among Charlemagne's friends. As early as 770 Charlemagne had behaved toward Tassilo in a crooked fashion ; and in the work of building his empire it was much to his advantage that Tassilo should be guilty of something. Seven years later Tassilo was dragged from his monastery, to appear before the Synod of Frankfort, where, publicly renouncing all claims to his dukedom, he received the forgiveness of Charlemagne and permission to return—to the prison from which he had been temporarily released for the purpose of this public humiliation.

Chapter XII

1 *Sclavis ... Wilzi ... Welatabi.* The Slavs were one of the most numerous of the branches of the Aryan family. The South-western branch had by this time spread over a great part of the Eastern Empire, between the Danube and the

NOTES: CHAPTERS XI. 1—XIII. 1

Peloponnese. The North-eastern Slavs covered what is now known as Russia, Poland and Bohemia, Brandenburg, and in general the country east of the Elbe. They were separated from the South-western branch by the Avars in Hungary. The Slavs were called by the Germans, *Wends*.

The Wilzi were a Wendish or Slavonic tribe living in what is now Western Pommerania.

2 *Abodritos*. The Abodrites were another Wendish tribe, in Northern Mecklenburg, about Wismar.

Sinus: the Baltic.

3 *Sueones*, the Swedes. The name 'Northmen' was not limited to the Swedes, but was applied by the Franks to the Scandinavian races in general. Einhard's knowledge of the races who lived round the Baltic is better than his knowledge of the sea itself. Actually the Baltic is 850 to 900 miles in length, and 100 to 200 miles wide.

Aisti: the Esthonians, themselves a Slavonic tribe.

una tantum ... expeditione: i.e. A.D. 789. The forces sent by Charlemagne laid waste the land of the Wilzi as far as the River Peene.

Chapter XIII

1 *Maximum omnium*. The Avars were a Turanian people, like their predecessors the Huns, and their successors the Magyars. Einhard loosely calls the Avars 'Huns'. After the Saxons, they were the most formidable foes of Charlemagne. The war was undertaken in 791 to protect Friuli and the frontiers of Bavaria from their inroads. In the expedition of this year, two armies took part: one, under Charlemagne himself, consisted of Franks, and marched down the right bank of the Danube (Pannonia); the other, consisting of Saxons and Frisians, under Theodoric and Maganfred, marched down the left bank.

maiori apparatu. The expedition was very carefully prepared. Ratisbon was the base for the forces. A service of boats kept up communications between the two armies on the right and left bank of the Danube, and supplied them with provisions.

The time consumed by this expedition was August and September, 791. Charlemagne was practically unopposed throughout his march through the Avar territory from the Enns to the Raab, where an epidemic caused the death of most of his horses. As usual, he laid waste the hostile country through which he passed. It is to this expedition that the origin of the later East Mark or Austria is considered to be due.

cetera filio suo Pippino. The Saxon revolt of 793 prevented Charlemagne from undertaking in person the rest of the war against the Avars. Pepin had already co-operated in the expedition of 791, by leading a force from Italy into the region of the rivers Save and Drave.

praefectis provinciarum. Pepin was assisted by Eric, Governor of Friuli, and Gerold, Governor of Bavaria, who after notable successes were killed (see below, § 4).

2   *regia Kagani*: *regia* is for *regia domus*; cp. xxii. 5. The 'royal abode of the Khan' of the Avars was called the Ringa (Hringus, Campus), a huge fortified camp, with nine concentric lines. Pepin stormed and sacked it in 795 and again in 796. It was situated somewhere about the region of the River Theiss. The booty was sent in 795 to Aix, where Charlemagne made a division of it among his followers, and also sent a portion to the Pope, Hadrian I.

3   *recordari*: passive only in mediaeval Latin.

4   *Tharsaticam*: Tersatto. Liburnia is the north-eastern coast of the Adriatic, below the peninsula of Istria. Istria, Liburnia, and Dalmatia were within the Carolingian Empire, but the maritime towns of these provinces acknowledged the rule of the Eastern Emperor at Constantinople (see xv. 4). Eric's death in 799 does not seem to have been connected with the Avar war. But Gerold's death in the same year, the last year of the war, was due to a revolt of the Avars, who after the capture of the Ring had acknowledged the dominion of Charlemagne, when their Khan, Tudun, had also been baptized.

Einhard truly says that the loss of life by the Avars in these wars was tremendous. They practically disappear from history at this point, and are merged in the Magyars, who followed them, a Turanian race, similar therefore in origin to the Avars. The Magyars, under the name of Hungarians, continued to trouble Middle Europe by their raids for another two centuries.

tametsi diutius . . ., 'although it dragged on a good deal longer than the importance of its operations justified'. *sui* should, in classical Latin, be *sua*.

5   *Boemanicum*. The war against the Bohemians took place in 805.

Linonicum. A Slavonic tribe, east of the Elbe, who took sides with the Danish king Gottfried in 808, and accordingly were devastated by a punitive expedition sent by Charlemagne.

Karoli iunioris. Charlemagne's eldest son. See Table, p. 63.

Chapter XIV

1 *Nordmannos qui Dani vocantur*: cp. chap. xii. **3**. From this time till the settlement of Normandy by the Treaty of St. Clair-sur-Epte in 911, this people was a terror to Northern Europe. In 810 Gottfried, the formidable King of Denmark, caused Charlemagne to undertake his last war. After piratical descents on Frisia, Gottfried was expected to attempt an invasion of Germany. He seems to have wielded a sort of imperial power in the North, and after the fashion of the Roman emperors had constructed (in 808) a great wall across Denmark, the famous 'Dannewerk', between the Baltic and the North Sea, where the country narrows, to the north of the river Eider. Charlemagne was actually leading an army against Gottfried, and had got as far as the River Weser, when he heard of Gottfried's assassination.

Chapter XV

2 *Ligerim*: the Loire.

oceanum: the Atlantic ocean, in this case really the Bay of Biscay.

mare Balearicum: the sea between the Balearic Islands and the mainland of Spain.

Thuringos: the Thuringians were a Saxon people.

Sorabos: the Sorbs were a Slavonic people, living between the Saale and the Elbe, and conquered by Charlemagne in 806. To preserve his conquest he built the fortresses of Halle and Magdeburg.

Alamanni: Alemannia, a province which included the later Duchy of Suabia. It lay between the Black Forest and the Lech. The names Suabians and Alemannians are used synonymously up till about A.D. 1000.

3 *Aquitaniam, Wasconiam*: see above, chap. v.

Hiberum amnem: the Ebro.

Dertosae civitatis: Tortosa.

Augusta Praetoria: Aosta.

Graecorum ac Beneventorum . . . confinia. Benevento was a Lombard duchy, settled by the Lombards (with Spoleto as another duchy) in the sixth century. During the next three and a half centuries the allegiance of Benevento was claimed by the Western Emperors, the Eastern Emperors, the Papacy, and the Normans of South Italy. After 1053 it was regarded as part of the Papal States.

Southern Italy or *Calabria* was reckoned as a 'Theme'

or province of the Eastern (Byzantine) Empire down till the conquest by the Normans of Apulia and Calabria, between 1042 and 1059.

et eius . . . duplum, 'double as broad as that part which the Franks occupy'. This gen. (*eius*) is not a classical usage.

4 *Pannoniam*. This was the old Roman province, between the Danube and the Save. Dacia was north of the Danube, and extended from the Black Sea on the east almost to the River Theiss on the west.

Histriam, etc.: cp. note to xiii. 4.

Constantinopolitanum imperatorem : see below, xvi. 4.

5 *deinde omnes*, etc. The main verb of this sentence is *perdomuit*.

Visulam: Vistula.

This chapter is the *locus classicus* for any description of the limits of Charlemagne's empire. It is a statement true only with certain qualifications. The region between the Ocean and the Balearic Sea, i.e. Gascony, did not really form part of the dominions of Pepin the Short, but was under its own native Duke, and was practically independent till 819. Brittany also was always under native Dukes. Aquitaine, on the contrary, was not really acquired by Charlemagne, but was already held by Pepin the Short; all that Charlemagne had to do was to meet a revolt in favour of the old Ducal family. Finally it must be noted that Einhard does not distinguish between (1) those portions of the Empire which were completely administered by Charlemagne and his officials ; (2) the more outlying regions, (e.g. the conquests from the Slavs), which were merely tributary; and (3) the domains left to the Pope. See Introd.

cum his : with the four peoples just mentioned.

ceteras, i.e. *barbaras, ac feras nationes* (above).

Chapter XVI

1 *Hadefonsum*. Alfonso II reigned from 789-842.

Galleciae atque Asturicae. Galicia in the north-west of Spain, and Asturias in the north, developed ultimately into the kingdom of Leon.

is: i.e. Alfonso.

eum: i.e. Charlemagne.

illum: i.e. Charlemagne.

proprium: cf. xiv, *fin*. 'proprio satellite'. 'To such an extent did he win the friendship of Alfonso, King of Galicia and Asturias, that whenever Alfonso sent him ambassadors or letters, he (Alfonso) would order he should

NOTES: CHAPTERS XV. 3—XVI. 4

be known at the Carolingian court only as Charlemagne's devoted friend.' In 798, Alfonso sent to Charlemagne a portion of the Moorish spoils taken at the sack of Lisbon.

2 *Scottorum . . . reges.* Scotti at this time means the Irish. Charlemagne sent envoys to Ireland who, returning through Mercia in 796, brought to him news of the death of Æthelred of Northumbria. *Epistolae Karolini Aevi,* ed. Duemmler, ii. 147.

3 *Aaron rege Persarum.* This was Harun al-Raschid, Caliph of Bagdad (786–809).

In 807 Harun al-Raschid sent an envoy called Abdella to Charlemagne, along with a deputation from the Christian monks of Jerusalem, who, although tolerated by Harun, were none the less anxious to have the countenance of the Western Emperor. Among the presents from Harun to Charlemagne was a water-clock which registered twelve hours. The recognition of Charlemagne by the Caliph as protector of the Christians in Jerusalem should be noted.

donariis, ' offerings ' : more usually the shrines at which they were made (as in chap. xxvii. **2**).

elephantum : its name was Abu-l-Abbas; its keeper one Isaac, a Jew; it died in 810.

4 *Nicephorus I* was Eastern (Byzantine) Emperor from 802–11 ; *Michael I,* 811–13 ; *Leo V,* 813–20. Charlemagne died before his ambassadors could bring word from Leo V, but Louis the Pious completed the negotiations.

As a whole, the relations of the Eastern Empire with Charlemagne had been anything but friendly. The two empires clashed in South Italy, particularly over the Duchy of Benevento. Nevertheless, Charlemagne had formed ideas for a marriage alliance between his family and the Byzantine imperial house. His daughter Rothrude was affianced in 781 to Constantine VI, but the marriage never took place (see chap. xix. **2**). In 801, Charlemagne, now a widower, offered to marry the regent Irene, mother of Constantine VI. But the revolution by which Nicephorus I came to the throne put an end to this proposal. The new Emperor was at first friendly, but in 806 he sent a fleet to recover the Dalmatian coast. Charlemagne's son, Pepin of Italy, met this expedition successfully, and in 807 concluded a truce. The war, renewed in 809, was again concluded by a truce in 810. In 811 an embassy from Nicephorus came to Aix-la-Chapelle, and a definite peace was arranged. Charlemagne renounced his claim to Venice and the Dalmatian coast-towns ; in return Nicephorus recognized him as Emperor. The next Byzantine ruler, Michael I, sent to Aix in the year of his accession an embassy which gave Charlemagne the style of 'Imperator' and 'Basileus' (*Annales Einhardi, sub anno* 812). It was of great importance for the Carolingian House to be thus recognized by the Eastern Emperors, who, having their authority direct from ancient Rome, were rightly held to be the most 'legitimate' Sovereigns in Christendom. There were now, therefore, two Emperors, an Eastern and a Western, ruling as formerly in the fifth century, with divided sway over the regions of the old Roman Empire.

ultro. This is a courtly version. Actually it was Charlemagne who was anxious for the friendship of the Eastern Empire.

Τὸν Φράγκον . . ., 'have the Frank for a friend, do not have him for a neighbour'.

The old hostility between Greeks and Franks amounted to racial aversion. The feeling was later very strong during the period of the Crusades. The suspicions of the Greeks were only too well justified by the Latin conquest of Constantinople in 1204. Religious differences may have had much to do with this feeling.

This chapter of Einhard is by no means complete in its account of the external relations of Charlemagne. It omits the important friendship with Offa, King of Mercia. Two letters of Charlemagne to Offa, one dated between 793 and 796, the other in 796, are printed in *Epistolae Karolini Aevi*, ed. Duemmler, ii. 131, 144. Einhard also omits the interesting fact that Egbert, King of the West Saxons, who reigned from 802 to 839, was an honoured refugee at Charlemagne's court from about the year 793, although his exile was largely brought about by Charlemagne's friend Offa of Mercia. See Henry of Huntingdon, *Historia Anglorum* (Rolls Series), p. 131.

Chapter XVII

2 *Mogontiacum*: Mainz (Mayence).

antequam decederet, 'before Charlemagne's death'.

conflagravit, 'was burned down'. The bridge was not rebuilt till the nineteenth century. The conflagration occurred in May 813 (*Ann. R. Franc., sub anno* 813).

3 *Ingilenheim*: Ingelheim, eight miles south-west of Mainz. For the historical frescoes in the Palace there see Poem of Ermold in *Poetae Latini Aevi Carolini*, ed. Duemmler, ii, pp. 63–4.

Noviomagi: Nimeguen.

Vahalem fluvium: the Waal, the principal arm of the Rhine Delta.

Batavorum insulam: Betuwa, a territory in Guelderland, between the Waal and Lek.

ut restaurarentur imperavit. For Charlemagne's policy of making the Churchmen do their duty in keeping up the fabrics of the churches, see the *Capitulare ad Salzi*, 804, in *M. G. H.*, Pertz, *Leges*, t. i, pp. 123-4 'Ut ecclesiae Dei bene constructae et restauratae fiant, et episcopi unusquisque infra suam parrochiam exinde bonam habeat providentiam'.

4 *aedificatis ... navibus*: the organization of sea-power against the Northmen, who for the next century were a scourge to Northern Europe, is the greatest possible evidence of the foresight and clearness of intellect of Charlemagne. In 800 a fleet and system of coast defence was organized for the West of France, under Louis of Aquitaine. In 811 a similar system of naval defence was instituted for the North. The great naval stations were Boulogne and Ghent.

Narbonensis ac Septimaniae. These words are synonymous. Narbonne was the chief town of the March of Septimania.

The Moors of Spain this time were making themselves felt as pirates in the Mediterranean. In 807 Charlemagne sent a strong fleet under Burchard, his Master of the Horse (*Comes stabuli*), to protect Corsica and Sardinia from the Moorish fleet. Burchard defeated the Moors, who lost thirteen ships, but next year they returned and overran most of Corsica.

Centumcellae: Civita Vecchia. This happened in 813. In the same year, shortly before, Irmingarius, Count of Empurias (in Catalonia), had captured eight Moorish ships off Majorca.

Chapter XVIII

1 *abhinc*, 'from this point'; not a classical usage.

Charlemagne was four times married; his legitimate children numbered eight: of these, all the three sons, and three of the daughters, were born from Hildegard, who was Charlemagne's favourite wife. The third daughter, Gisla, and the two daughters of Fastrada became abbesses. Rothrude and Bertha, like Gisla and their two half-sisters, seem to have been prevented from marrying by Charlemagne: see below, chap. xix, *ad fin*. (Introd., pp. xxvi-xxvii).

2 *Suaborum*: Suabians (see above, note to chap. xv. 2).

3 *nomen.* It was probably Sigradane : *modo,* ' at the moment '.

Defuncta Fastrada. She died in 794, Liutgard died six years later.

Madelgardam . . . Ruothildem. One MS. only has this clause, but there is no reason to suppose it otherwise than genuine.

Drogonem: became Archbishop of Metz (from 823–55).

Hugum: became Abbot of St. Quentin (died 844).

4 *invicem,* ' between them '.

apud Sanctum Dionysium: St. Denis, four miles north of Paris. Since the seventh century the burying place of the Kings of France, although Charlemagne was not buried there. It is not known, however, what his intentions were for his own burial. See chap. xxxi. 1.

CHAPTER XIX

1 *quibus et ipse operam dabat.* Charlemagne was not really educated, being unable to write. (But he could read, although he seems usually to have been read to, and he collected a good library; cp. chaps. xxv. 3, xxxiii. 9.) He was anxious to give his children the advantages which had been denied to himself.

venatibus : for the more usual ' venationibus ' (which is found in one of our MSS.).

2 *Bernhardum*: Bernhard was King of Italy from 813–17.

4 *Adequitabant ei* : rode with (or beside) him.

pone : just behind.

contubernio : their society.

5 The last two sentences of this chapter, omitted by our best MSS., may very possibly be a subsequent addition (by Einhard or by some one else). See Introd., p. viii.

fortunae malignitatem. Rothrude formed an irregular union with Count Rorigo, and had a son, Louis, Abbot of St. Denis. Bertha also formed an irregular union, with the poet Angilbert, and had a son, the historian Nithard : See *M. G. H.*, Pertz, i. 474 (*Hincmari Ann.*) and ii. 671 (*Nithardi Hist.*).

The story of a connexion between Einhard himself and Charlemagne's daughter Emma is, no doubt, a myth. (Einhard's wife was called Emma.)

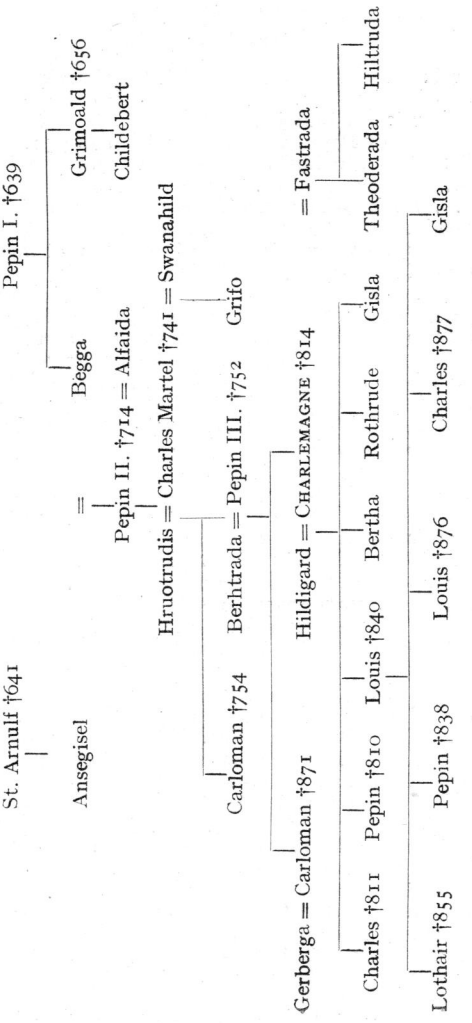

THE ANCESTORS, CHILDREN, AND GRANDCHILDREN OF CHARLEMAGNE.

Chapter XX

1 *Pippinus* : not to be confused with Charlemagne's second son, Pepin of Italy.
gibbo deformis : a hunchback.
The rebellion of Pepin was in the winter of 792.
Prumia: Prüm, in Lotharingia, about thirty miles north of Treves.

2 *alia . . . coniuratio* : the Thuringian rebellion, 785–6. The ringleader was one Hardrad.
luminibus orbati : for this form of punishment in England in the twelfth century see Stubbs, *Charters* (ed. Davis), p. 115, A. D. 1124.

3 *exorbitasse*, 'had turned aside from'. The record of the Saxon wars might be considered to require some modification in this statement. In 782, Charlemagne had 4,500 of the Saxon rebels hung in one day at Verden, on the Aller. But they had been guilty of destroying churches and driving out the priests. This act of cruelty took place *before* the union with Fastrada.

Chapter XXI

1 *suscipiendis*, 'maintaining'.
non inmerito, 'with some show of reason'. There seems to be here some note of personal annoyance. If so, there are two persons who may be suggested as possibly the objects of this slighting reference. One is the unnamed Irish scholar (' Scottus '), at whose head Einhard sometimes felt the temptation of hurling books and furniture, and whom he is supposed to have described inelegantly as 'a sot, and no Scot' (Theodulfus, *Ad Karl. Reg.* 159–60). The other is Paulus Diaconus. The stories of Paulus' treachery towards Charlemagne are very likely no more than legend, in their detail. But they seem to point to the fact that he left the court under some cloud ; and it is perhaps significant that Einhard in chap. xxv. **2** (if the text there be sound) omits from the list of scholars who adorned Charles' reign the historian and lexicographer who, after Alcuin, was the principal literary figure of the time.

The Monk of S. Gall mentions (i. 5), a humble clerk of the Palace School on whom Charlemagne ' had compassion ' —'licet omnes eum odio haberent et *expellere niterentur*'.

Among distinguished foreigners of a different order who found a refuge at Charlemagne's court, the most notable was Egbert, King of the Saxons. Such a visitor, no doubt,

NOTES: CHAPTERS XX. 1—XXIII

brought with him a considerable retinue—who would tend to be *onerosi*.

2 *prae*, 'in accordance with'; classical Latin would require *pro*.

NB

Chapter XXII

1 *iustam*: sc. *staturam*.

nam septem . . . mensuram, 'it is allowed that his height was equal to seven times the length of his own foot'. As we do not know the length of Charlemagne's foot, we are not much the wiser—we have no such assistance as enabled Pythagoras to discover the length of Heracles' foot. The average foot of a man, however, is said to be eleven inches. This would give Charlemagne a height of six feet, five inches.

vegetis, 'bright', 'quick'.

canitie pulchra, 'with white hair which became him'.

2 *unde . . . adquirebatur*, 'from all these characteristics his appearance won a very great dignity and impressiveness, whether he stood or sat'.

obesa et brevior, 'thick and rather short'. Theodulf, on the other hand, praises the beauty of Charlemagne's neck, *Ad Kar. Reg.* 17.

proiectior, 'protruding'.

aequalitas, 'excellent proportion'.

treble

3 *voce . . . conveniret*. The meaning seems to be that his voice was loud, though hardly so loud as one would expect in a man of such large frame.

claudicaret. Charlemagne seems to have suffered from the gout; the waters of Apollo Grannus at Aix (Aquae Grani), were employed by him as a 'cure': see below, 5. 6-8.

4 *assa*, 'roast meats'.

elixis, 'boiled meats'.

Chapter XXIII

This chapter should be read in connexion with the account of the Frankish dress given by the Monk of S. Gall (i. 34):

'Erat antiquorum ornatus vel paratura Francorum: calciamenta forinsecus aurata, corrigiis tricubitalibus insignita, fasciolae crurales vermiculatae, et subtus eas tibialia, vel coxalia, linea, quamvis ex eodem colore tamen opere artificiosissimo variata; super quae et fasciolas in crucis modum, intrinsecus et extrinsecus, ante et retro, longissimae illae corrigiae tendebantur; deinde camisia clizana ; post haec balteus spate colligatus, quae spata primum vagina, secundo corio qualicunque, tertio lintheamine candidissimo cera lucidissima roborato ita cingebatur ut per medium cruciculis eminentibus ad peremptionem gentilium duraretur. Ultimum habitus eorum erat pallium canum vel sapphirinum, quadrangulum, duplex, sic formatum ut, cum imponeretur umeris, ante et retro pedes tangeret, de lateribus vero vix genua contegeret.'

The good monk was 'lazy as a tortoise', as he tells us, and never went abroad. But he had seen the King of the Franks so dressed in S. Gall itself.

1 *camisam lineam*: understand some such word as *gerebat* (*ad corpus*, 'next to his skin'): the *camisa* is the French 'chemise'.

feminalia are drawers (*femur, feminis*, the thigh).

limbo serico, 'a silk border'.

tibialia: must be stockings (not leggings—as Hodgkin, *Italy*, viii. 128), for over these *tibialia* he wore *fasciolae* (= puttees). This appears more clearly from the *Monk of S. Gall* (quoted above).

Very long and elaborate *fasciae* were considered luxurious and effeminate: Alcuin, *Ep.* 34, Duemmler.

ex pellibus lutrinis et murinis thorace confecto, 'with a waistcoat made of otter-skin and ermine' (*lutra*, an otter: *mures*, martens or ermines): *thorace*, a kind of waistcoat, or pelisse. Einhard takes the word from Suet. *Aug.* 82.

sago veneto, 'a soldier's blue cloak', the 'pallium sapphirinum' of the *Monk of S. Gall*.

Chapter XXIV

1 *quaternis tantum ferculis*, 'consisting of only four courses'.

2 *acroama*. The word means originally any gratification of the ear: then, any person affording such gratification. It may be here either a *singer* or a *court-jester*.

lectorem. The *Monk of S. Gall*, i. 7, has an interesting account of the readings at Charlemagne's court, and of Charlemagne's treatment of his readers.

De Civitate Dei. There is no reason to doubt that this book coloured Charlemagne's whole conception of the Empire, and that it was one of the deepest influences in his politico-religious thinking.

super cenam, 'at meals'.

eius = *Karoli*: *ipsius* would be more correct: but cf. *suis* for *eius*, chap. 17 *fin*.

NOTES: CHAPTERS XXIII. 1—XXV. 2

4 *nec hoc tantum . . . expediebat*, 'nor did he behave like this merely at the time of dressing himself, but whenever any kind of business presented itself later in the day, or when orders had to be given to officials, he discharged the matter with the same improvised efficiency'.

Chapter XXV

1 *orare*, 'to pray': the passage is very interesting in the light which it throws on Einhard's method of borrowing from Suetonius (see Introd., pp. xxvii sqq.). It is modelled upon Suet. *Titus* 3 'Latine Graeceque vel in orando vel in fingendis poematibus promptus', where, however, *orando* means not 'prayer', but, as often in Latin, 'oratory', 'public speaking'.
pronuntiare, merely 'to speak', not 'to pronounce'.
dicaculus, 'wordy'.

2 *Artes liberales*. The literary revival of the age of Charlemagne is a phenomenon hardly less important in its consequences to Europe than the foundation of the Empire itself. To it we owe (1) the preservation of nearly all the remains of ancient Latin literature which we possess, and (2) the handwriting—and thence the typography—still employed by the peoples of Western Europe. Literature as such was not Charlemagne's primary concern, when he undertook the reform of Education. He was interested primarily in religion, and he desired a thorough revision of biblical, liturgical, and ecclesiastical texts—all of which had become deeply corrupted. The monasteries, which should have been a last refuge of Learning, contained, many of them, monks who could neither read, write, nor do simple arithmetic. Those of them who *could* write wrote a script almost wholly illegible, were unable to spell, and had the most distant acquaintance with the Latin language. This condition of things Charlemagne resolved to end. He wanted good texts, before anything else, of the books of the Church, and men who understood these texts. But he perceived—as more enlightened enthusiasts have sometimes failed to perceive—and he emphasized in his capitulary *De Litteris Colendis*[1], the need of a general culture before the literature which the Church primarily valued could be truly understood. Of the three men who were the chief instruments of his reform, two are here mentioned by Alcuin. The third was Paulus Diaconus (?725–97), whose History of the Lombards is one of our primary sources for the knowledge of that people, but who is perhaps even better known

[1] See the full text, printed on pp. xxxix–xl.

by his abridgement of the Lexicon of Festus. For the omission of his name in this chapter see on xxi. 1. (His Letters are collected in Duemmler, *Epp. Kar. Aev.* ii. 506 sqq.)

Two other members of the Palace School who deserve mention here are the poets Angilbert and Theodulf. To the latter we owe a highly interesting picture of the literary circle which surrounded Charlemagne (the poem *Ad Karolum Regem*, Duemmler, *Poet. Aev. Kar.* i. 483 sqq.).

Petrum Pisanum. Little is known of him. He is called elsewhere 'Peter the grammarian', 'Petrus magister'. A letter of Alcuin (112) tells us of a rivalry of wit between him and Paulus.

Albinum. Alcuin of York was born probably in 735. In 768 he visited Charlemagne at Aix-la-Chapelle. He met the emperor again at Parma in 781, and was induced to take up his residence in the Palace School, over which he seems to have presided until 790. In 793 he was made Abbot of Tours. It was at Tours that he helped to develop in the writing-schools the script known as the Caroline minuscule.[1] He died at Tours in 804. He was without doubt one of the principal influences in Charlemagne's life, and supplied wise direction and counsel not only in matters of education, but in both civil and ecclesiastical politics.

astronomiae means, it is to be feared, no more than *astrologiae*. For Charlemagne's interest in Astrology see on xxxiii. 10.

3 *conputandi*, 'calculating'. Mere arithmetic was not a general accomplishment at the time. But by *conputandi* is to be understood here the elaborate calculations required for astrology.

scribere. Gibbon is probably right when he says that the plain meaning of these words is that 'in his mature age the emperor strove to acquire the practice of writing —which every peasant now learns in his infancy'. Others have understood it of the ornamental literary writing now just coming into use under the influence of Alcuin. This is hardly consistent with *tabulas et codicillos* below—materials not suited for such writing (to say nothing of the difficulty of writing ornamentally *in bed*). Charlemagne, no doubt, sought to acquire the ordinary cursive hand of the day—the illegible script which we call ' Merovingian '.

cervicalibus, ' pillows ', ' cushions '.

---

[1] For a singularly beautiful specimen of Caroline handwriting see the frontispiece to this book, which reproduces a page of a Sacramentary written for Charlemagne's son Drogo, Archbishop of Metz.

Chapter XXVI

1 *basilicam* : the Chapel of the Virgin, to which Aix-la-Chapelle owes a part of its name. The most important part of this church still survives. It was built under the direction of a certain Otho (there is no ground for connecting Einhard with the building : the tradition that he was an architect seems to rest on a misunderstanding). It was opened by Pope Leo III on January 6, 805. Imitated from the Church of S. Vitalis in Vienna, it has little real pretension to architectural beauty or distinction (Lavisse, *Hist. de France*, 1. ii, p. 351).

luminaribus, 'candelabra', not 'windows'. Cf. *Capitul.* Pertz, p. 123, 1.

2 *sacrificii*. The Eucharist; 'sacrificium dictum quasi sacrum factum, quia prece mystica consecratur in memoriam pro nobis Dominicae Passionis; unde hoc eo iubente corpus Christi et sanguinem dicimus', Isidore, *Etym.* vi. 19. 38.

aedituos, ' aedituus, aedis sacrae tuitor ', Paulus Diaconus.

ianitoribus = *ostiariis*. See Isidore, *Etym.* vii. 12. 32 'ostiarii idem et ianitores, qui in Veteri Testamento electi sunt ad custodiam templi, ut non ingrederetur eum inmundus in omni re. Dicti autem ostiarii, quod praesint ostiis templi.'

3 *psallendi disciplinam*. Charlemagne brought with him from Rome in 786 trained Italian choir-masters, who at Metz and Soissons instructed the choristers of various Frankish churches. See the *Monk of S. Gall*, i, chap. 10, and Ioh. Diac. *Vita S. Greg.* ii. 9. 10.

admodum, ' quite '.

Chapter XXVII

1 *transmarinorum regum amicitias*: cp. chap. xvi. 3 'Aaron rege Persarum ' ; and notes.

refrigerium : common in mediaeval Latin. It came into the language of literature from the Biblical Latin.

2 *ecclesiam beati Petri* : the Basilica of St. Peter, which occupied the site of the Vatican till the sixteenth century.

3 *antiquius*, ' more important ' ; a prior consideration (as often in Cicero).

quater : Charlemagne was in Rome in 774, 781, 787, 800.

Chapter XXVIII

1 *iniuriis.* On April 25, 799, Leo III, as he was riding in procession to the Church of St. Laurence, was attacked by a band of bravoes, incited by Paschalis and Campulus, the nephews of the late Pope Hadrian. The conspirators left Leo lying in a church, after attempting to put out his eyes and cut out his tongue. This mutilation, if effected, would legally have incapacitated him from holding the Papacy or, indeed, any priestly office. Leo recovered from the brutal attack, and his escape from permanent blindness was considered to be a miracle.

2 *aversatus est*: an attitude of *nolo regere, nolo episcopari*, was exacted by the rules of polite society in the Middle Ages. It is probably true, however, that Charlemagne hoped to set the imperial crown on his own head, and was surprised when, while he was praying in front of the altar, Leo suddenly crowned him. But Charlemagne can hardly have been unaware when he went into St. Peter's on December 25, to be present at the Christmas Mass, that he was to be acclaimed as emperor.

Romanis imperatoribus: the Eastern emperors. See chap. xvi. **4**, and notes. Actually, in 800, when Charlemagne became Western emperor, the Empress Irene was ruling alone at Constantinople.

fratres. From the point of view of the Eastern emperors, it was not magnanimity but presumption in Charlemagne, to address them as brothers.

epistolis. See *Monumenta Carolina* (Jaffé), p. 393, Charlemagne to Nicephorus I, and p. 415 to Michael I.

Chapter XXIX

1 *Post susceptum imperiale nomen.* The idea of a code of imperial laws had come down from the time of the Emperor Justinian. This passage in Einhard is the only evidence that Charlemagne thought of such a code. He certainly never carried out the idea. His empire was made up of various States, and each retained its old laws.

duas ... leges. The two systems of law were the code of the Salian Franks and that of the Ripuarian Franks. Salic was the name given by the Romans to the Franks who occupied the Lower Rhine and the Lower Meuse. The Ripuarians inhabited the Middle Rhine, chiefly the district round Cologne.

NOTES: CHAPTERS XXVIII. 1—XXIX. 3

perperam prolata, ' wrongly edited '. Laws were originally unwritten customs. When they were defined and put into writing, mistakes or misinterpretations were apt to occur.

pauca capitula. Charlemagne left the ancient laws of these two peoples, but made certain additions to them in 803 (*M. G. H.*, Pertz, *Leges*, i, pp. 112, 117).

2 *Omnium ... nationum.* This does not include all the nations which Einhard (chap. xv) reckoned as being under the dominion of Charlemagne. Only the customs of those which were directly administered by Charlemagne's officials were thus edited, the Saxons, the Thuringians, the Frisians.

barbara. German, as contrasted with Latin. Several collections of the vernacular songs and poems of minstrels, as sung and recited in the halls of the Frankish kings, were made in the eighth and ninth centuries. But these collections, including that of Charlemagne, have completely disappeared. Only one considerable fragment of pre-Christian Old High German poetry has survived, the *Hildebrandslied*, an epic which was written down by the monks of Einhard's own monastery of Fulda, at the beginning of the ninth century, and of which the greater portion has survived. Old High German was the language of the Upper Rhine, of the Alemannians and Bavarians, and also of the Franks. Charlemagne's court spoke it.

Inchoavit et grammaticam patrii sermonis, ' he made some attempt to found also a scholarship of the German tongue '.

grammaticam means ' grammar ', or ' philology ', in the wide sense of the word, but it *may* also mean a definite text-book of grammar.

3 *propriam linguam,* ' his native tongue '; cp. above, *patrii sermonis.* The separation between Old High German, which the Franks now spoke, and the Low German, of the Lower Rhine, took place early in the seventh century. Old High German has become the literary language of Germany. The dividing line between Old High German and Low German ran from Aix-la-Chapelle through Düsseldorf to about Magdeburg. The Dutch tongue and ' Platt-deutsch ' come from Low German.

barbaris. German, as in § 2.

Hornung. ' Horn ' in Old High German means *corner.* The meaning of ' Hornung ' is obscure. Perhaps like the Latin ' January ', it was considered as looking both to the past and coming years.

Lentzinmanoth : spring month ; our word *Lent.*

Ostarmanoth : Easter month.

Winnemanoth : love month.

Brachmanoth : when the land is broken up.

Heuuimanoth : hay month.
Aranmanoth : harvest month.
Witumanoth : wood month.
Windumemanoth : vine-gathering month.
Herbistmanoth : autumn month (our word *harvest*).
Heilagmanoth : holy month.

CHAPTER XXX

1 *solus filiorum*. Pepin of Italy died on July 8, 810. Charles died in 811. In 813, Charlemagne made his last legitimate son, Louis of Aquitaine, emperor with himself, not so much in order that Louis might share in the Imperial functions (for he immediately returned to Aquitaine), but in order that the succession to the Empire, on Charlemagne's death, might be assured. The taking of a colleague on the throne had been a custom of the ancient Roman emperors, and it was also the practice of the early Capetian kings of France, who succeeded the House of Charlemagne after 987.

congregatis . . . primoribus. This was one of the General Assemblies or Synods, which had been held from time to time by Pepin the Short and Charlemagne. Although probably all the people were supposed to attend, only the great laymen and ecclesiastics were actually summoned. The Assembly of Aix-la-Chapelle took place in September 813; besides approving of the choice of a colleague for the emperor, the Assembly also passed a Capitulary of forty-six articles (*M. G. H.*, Pertz, *Leges*, i. 187). The consent of *omnes fideles Christianae ecclesiae* is mentioned, as well as of the bishops and counts. The coronation of Louis, which Charlemagne performed himself without any intervention of Pope or bishop, took place in the great Church of Aix, on Sunday, September 11.

2 *inspiratum* : another trace of Biblical Latin.

venatum, 'to hunt'. This, with bathing and swimming in the great baths at Aix-la-Chapelle, was the chief recreation of Charlemagne.

3 *decubuit*, 'took to his bed'. This was on January 22.

Qui, 'he', i. e. Charlemagne.

rarissimo potu, 'a very occasional draught of water'. Charlemagne thought to reduce his fever by starving himself.

sacra communione percepta : the regular mediaeval phrase.

V. Kal. Feb. Charlemagne died on January 28, at 9 a.m.

Chapter XXXI

1 *lotum et curatum*, 'washed and prepared for burial'. *curatum* has sometimes been taken here to mean embalmed (e.g. Lavisse, *Hist. de France*, i. 330), but as Charlemagne was interred on the same day as he died (*eadem die qua et defunctus est*, below, § 2), there can hardly have been time for embalming. Suetonius uses *curare* for 'to lay out a body', to prepare it for burial (*Nero*, 49).

2 *eadem die.* It was perhaps because Charlemagne was interred so soon after death, before any decay of the flesh could take place, that his body is said to have been found in such a good state of preservation when the Emperor Otto III opened up the tomb in 1000. It is said that Otto went down into a vault of the church at Aix-la-Chapelle with two bishops and a count, and found Charlemagne, who had not been buried, but walled in, seated on a chair. His crown was on his head, and his sceptre in his hands; his nails protruded through the fingers of the gloves which he wore. His flesh was perfectly preserved, except that the tip of his nose had decayed away. Otto and his three attendants fell on their knees before the seated figure of the great emperor. They then put new white clothes on the body, and had the tip of the nose restored with gold and one tooth extracted and taken away. After that, the body, still seated majestically, was walled up in its tomb (*Chronicon Novaliciense*, iii. 32, *M. G. H.*, Pertz, ix. 106).

When the tomb is next known to have been re-opened, in 1165, the body was found in a marble sarcophagus. Accordingly, doubt has been thrown on the story of Otto III. It is also difficult to understand how the body of Charlemagne, if not embalmed, could be so well preserved, even in an air-tight chamber, after a lapse of one hundred and eighty-six years. Moreover, no traces of a vault have been discovered in the church at Aix (Davis, p. 309).

The bones of the emperor are still in a shrine in the church at Aix.

conditorio : tomb.

orthodoxi imperatoris. This is a challenge to the Eastern emperors, who, although they could trace their authority directly back to the ancient Roman emperor, were 'schismatic' in their religious observances.

septuagenarius : cp. above, chap. xxx, § 3 *septuagesimo secundo.* There is some vagueness about the date of Charlemagne's birth. *Septuagenarius* is perhaps used somewhat loosely here, as when we call a man a 'septuagenarian'.

The *Annales Lauriss.* say he died in his seventy-first year, (*sub anno* 814), see notes on chap. iv.

indictione septima. The indictions consisted of a revolution of fifteen years, each year being separately reckoned as indiction 1, indiction 2, &c., up to 15, when they recommence with indiction 1 (Harris Nicolas, *Chronology of History, The Indictions*).

There are four kinds of indictions: (1) The Constantinople, instituted by Constantine in 314; it began on September 1. (2) The Caesarean, beginning on September 24; (3) Roman or Pontifical, beginning on December 25 or January 1, 'accordingly as either of these days was considered the first of the year.' (4) The Paris indiction, beginning in October, used by the Parlements of Paris.

Charlemagne used both the Constantinople and the Roman Indiction. As Charlemagne died on January 28, which would be the same indiction, whether the Constantinople or the Roman reckoning were employed, it is impossible to say which Einhard is using here.

A safe method of finding the indiction of any day of the year which falls between January 1 and September 1, is to add 3 to the given year, and then to divide the sum by 15. If nothing remains over, the indiction of that year will be 15. If any number remains, that will be the number of the indiction; e. g. to find the indiction of Charlemagne's death (January 28, 814):

$$
\begin{array}{r}
814 \\
3 \\
\hline
15)817(54 \\
75 \\
\hline
67 \\
60 \\
\hline
7
\end{array}
$$

The seventh indiction is therefore the one in which he died.

Chapter XXXII

1 *sentiret,* ' was sensible of the threat of it '.

Per tres continuos . . . defectio. Not quite exact. The eclipses fell in the years 810, 812, 813. The two eclipses of 810 caused some perturbation in Charlemagne. See the letter which Dungal, ' recluse of St. Denis at Paris,' wrote to him (*Monumenta Carolina,* Jaffé, p. 396).

Porticus. Charlemagne built a covered way or colonnade between his palace and the great Church of Aix. After the colonnade fell down, it must have been rebuilt, as Otto the Great was elected King of the Germans in it in 936 (Witikind, ii. 1).

2 *hastula*: a spar or stick, lit. a little spear or branch (Ellis on Catullus, xvii).

For this bridge cp. chap. xvii, § 2.

3 *ultimam . . . expeditionem*: 810.

caelitus, ' from heaven '.

facem: a species of meteor. The ancients distinguished *faces, globi, trabes.*

capite deorsum merso, ' headfirst ', lit. its head collapsing downwards.

laqueariorum: ceilings ornamented with panels or fretwork. The panel-work began to shift and to fit badly, and so creaked.

4 *in margine coronae,* ' on the border of the circle which ran round the interior, between the upper and the lower arches '.

sinopide: in red. Red ochre was found at Sinope.

Chapter XXXIII

1 *Testamenta*: this refers to bequests of land, counties, and rights secured upon land. Charlemagne had only one lawful son left, Louis, who was now assured of the succession to the Empire. But his daughters were not provided for, either by land or marriage. Their only legitimate resource was the cloister. In the same way, Charlemagne made no permanent provision for his illegitimate children. This was probably deliberate on his part. He did not wish to set up a caste of royal princes, endowed with great lands and administrative privileges. He preferred that they should go into monasteries, and so die out. Charlemagne's views have had some justification in history. The system of ' appanaging ' the junior members of royal families brought rebellion and civil war in the later Middle Ages into France, Germany, and England.

76 VITA KAROLI

rata, 'assured', 'confirmed'.

breviario, 'a memorandum'.

5 *metropoleon* = μητροπολέων, an adjective, 'the metropolitan cities'.

Mediolanum : Milan.

Forum Iulii : Friuli.

Gradus : Grado, on the Adriatic, between Venice and Trieste.

Colonia : Cologne.

Mogontiacus : Mainz.

Iuvavum quae et Salzburg. The ancient Roman town of Iuvavum, after being practically destroyed by the Goths and Huns, was refounded under the name of Salzburg. The archbishopric was founded as late as 798.

Treveri : Treves.

Senones : Sens, in Champagne.

Vesontio : Besançon.

Lugdunum : Lyons.

Ratumagus : Rouen.

Remi : Rheims.

Arelas : Arles.

Vienna : Vienne, on the Rhone, south of Lyons.

Darantasia : Tarantaise, in Savoy.

Ebrodunum : Embrun, on the River Durance, in Dauphiny.

Burdigala : Bordeaux.

Turones : Tours.

Bituriges : Bourges.

7 *voluntariam secularium rerum carentiam* : this seems to imply that Charlemagne perhaps contemplated ending his life in a monastery. The word *carentiam* is purely mediaeval.

8 *cortinae*, 'curtains' (O.F. *cortine*); ecclesiastical Latin.

stragula : coverlets, rugs.

tapetia : tapestries, carpets.

filtra : woollen cloths.

coria, 'skins of beasts'.

sagmata, 'movables'.

erogatio eleemosynae, 'a charitable donation'.

9 *Capellam* : the plate and other goods for use in religious buildings and services. The word 'chapel' is here used for the ornaments which the building contained, just as we now use 'library' for the books which the library building contains.

tam . . . quam, 'both . . . and'.

conlata, 'which he had not made over as a gift to the *capella*'.

NOTES: CHAPTER XXXIII. 1-11

bibliotheca: for MSS. collected under Charlemagne's patronage see Introd., p. xli.

10 *tres mensas*: the earliest known maps were made of metal; cp. Herodotus, v. 49, where Aristagoras of Miletus took to Sparta a bronze plate, with the face of the earth and its seas and rivers engraven thereon (499 B.C.).

tribus orbibus connexa. This table, here described only very vaguely and obscurely, is spoken of more fully in the *St. Bertin Annals*, p. 438, Pertz 'disco etiam mirae magnitudinis ac pulchritudinis argenteo, in quo et orbis totius descriptio et astrorum consideratio et varius planetarum discursus, divisis ab invicem spatiis, signis eminentioribus sculpta radiabant.' From this it appears that the table was a silver planisphere, consisting of three concentric circles, of which the inner one (a) represented the Cosmos (Earth and the Heavens, *orbis totius descriptio*), the outer one (c), the firmament (*astrorum consideratio*), and the intermediate one (b), the motions of the planets. In other words, we have a rough description of the Ptolemaic system, in which $a=$ the Cosmos, $b=$ the seven spheres of Sun, Moon and planets, $c=$ the eighth sphere, that of the fixed stars (the system of *ten* spheres was not in use till four centuries later). In Charlemagne's time Bagdad, under Haroun al-Raschid, was the principal centre of astronomical knowledge; and the Carolingian interest in the heavens may owe something to Arabian influence.

Louis the Pious had specially reserved this table for himself from among his father's treasures (Thegan, viii); but in 842 the unfilial Lothair carried it off, broke it to bits, and paid his soldiers with the pieces.

11 *Hildibaldus*: Archbishop of Cologne. He was Arch-Chaplain, and administered the last sacrament to Charlemagne.

Richolfus: Archbishop of Mainz.

Arn: Archbishop of Salzburg.

Wolfarius: Archbishop of Rheims.

Bernoinus: Archbishop of Besançon.

Laidradus: Archbishop of Lyons. (See Introd., p. liv.)

Iohannes: Archbishop of Arles.

Theodulfus: Bishop of Orleans. (See Introd., p. liv.)

Iesse: Bishop of Amiens.

Heito: Bishop of Basle.

Waltgaudus: Bishop of Laon.

Fridugisus: Abbot of St. Bertin, Bertincourt (in Pas-de-Calais).

Adalungus: Abbot of St. Vedast, St. Waast, in Arras.

Engilbertus: Abbot of St. Riquier on the Somme.

Irmino: Abbot of St. Germain-des-Prés.

INDICES[1]

(a) INDEX OF PLACES AND PEOPLES

(WITH MODERN EQUIVALENTS OF THE LATIN PLACE-NAMES)

Abodriti, xii. 2 ; xiv. 2 ; xv. 5.
Aegyptus, xxvii. 1.
Africa, xxvii. 1.
Aisti, the Esthonians, xii. 3.
Alamanni, xi. 2 ; xv. 2.
Albis, *the Elbe*, vii. 5.
Alexandria, xxvii. 1.
Alpes, vi. 3.
Aquaegrani, *Aix-la-Chapelle (Aachen)*, xiv. 2 ; xvii. 2 ; xxii. 5 ; xxvi. 1 ; xxx. 2.
Aquitania, ii. 2 ; iii. 1 ; v. 2 ; vi. 1.
Arelas, *Arles*, xxxiii. 5.
Asturica, *the Asturias*, xvi. 1.
Augusta Praetoria, *Aosta*, xv. 3.
Avares, xiii. 1.

Baioaria, *Bavaria*, xi. 2 ; xiii. 4 ; xx. 1.
Baioarii, xi. 1 ; xv. 2.
Balaearicum Mare, xv. 2.
Batavi, xvii. 3.
Beneventani, x. 2 ; x. 3.
Birra, *the Berre*, ii. 2.
Bituriges, *Bourges*, xxxiii. 5.
Boemani, *Bohemians*, xv. 5.
Brittania, *Britain*, xxv. 2.
Brittones, *Bretons*, x. 1.
Burdigala, *Bordeaux*, xxxiii. 5.

Calabria, xv. 3.
Campania, x. 2.
Capua, x. 2.
Casinum Castrum, *Monte Cassino*, ii. 4.

Centumcellae, *Civita Vecchia*, xvii. 5.
Colonia, *Cologne*, xxxiii. 5.

Dacia, xv. 4.
Dalmatia, xv. 4.
Dani, xii. 3 ; xiv. 1 ; xxxii. 3.
Danubius, xv. 2 ; xv. 4.
Darantasia, *Tarantaise*, xxxiii. 5.
Dertosa, *Tortosa*, xv. 3.

Ebrodunum, *Embrun*, xxxiii. 5.
Etruria, xvii. 5.

Forum Iulii, *Friuli*, xxxiii. 5.
Frisia, xiv. 2 ; xvii. 5.
Fulda, *Walahfridi Prol.* 2.

Gallecia, xvi. 1.
Garonna, *the Garonne*, v. 2.
Gradus, *Grado*, xxxiii. 5.

Hasa, *the Haase*, viii. 1.
Hiberus, *the Ebro*, xv. 3.
Hierosolima, *Jerusalem*, xxvii. 1.
Hispania, ii. 2.
Histria, xv. 4.
Huni, xi. 1 ; xiii. 1-4.

India, xvi. 3.
Ingilenheim, *Ingelheim*, xvii. 3.
Iuvavum, *Salzburg*, xxxiii. 5.

Kartago, xxvii. 1.

---

[1] The Roman figures refer to *chapters*, the Arabic to *sections*. A few names of constant occurrence (*Franci, Galli, Itali, Romani*) are omitted from this Index.

INDEX OF PLACES AND PEOPLES

Langobardi, *Lombards*, iii. 4; vi. 1, 4; xviii. 2.
Lechus, *the Lech*, xi. 2.
Liburnia, xiii. 4.
Ligeris, *the Loire*, xv. 2.
Linones, xiii. 5.
Lugdunum, *Lyon*, xxxiii. 5.

Mauri, xvii. 5.
Meroingi, i. 1.
Moguntiacus, *Mainz (Mayence)*, xvii. 2, 3; xxxii. 2; xxxiii. 5.
Moingeuui, *Walafridi Prol.*, 2.

Narbona, *Narbonne*, ii. 2.
Narbonensis Provincia, xvii. 5.
Navarri, xv. 3.
Nordmanni, xii. 3; xiv. 1; xvii. 4; xvii. 5.
Noviomagus, *Nimeguen*, xvii. 3.

Osneggus, *Mt. Osning*, viii. 1.

Pannonia, xiii. 1, 4; xv. 4.
Parisii, *Paris*, iii. 1.
Persae, xvi. 3.
Pictavium, *Poitiers*, ii. 2.
Prumia, *Prüm*, xx. 1.
Pyrineus Mons, ix. 1; xv. 3.

Ratumagus, *Rouen*, xxxiii. 5.
Ravenna, xxvi. 1; xxxiii. 5; xxxv. 10.
Remi, *Rheims*, xxxiii. 5.

Rhenus, *the Rhine*, xv. 2; xv. 5; xvii. 2; xxxii. 2.

Sala, *the Saale*, xv. 2.
Salzburg, xxxiii. 5.
Samnium, *the Abruzzi*, ii. 4.
Sarraceni, ii. 2.
Sclavi, xii. 1, 3.
Scotti, *the Irish*, xvi. 2.
Senones, *Sens*, xxxiii. 5.
Septimania, xvii. 5.
Sorabi, xv. 2; xv. 5.
Soracte, *St. Oreste*, ii. 2.
Suabi, xviii. 2.
Sueones, *the Swedes*, xii. 3.
Syria, xxvii. 1.

Tharsatica, *Tersatto*, xiii. 4.
Theotmellus, *Detmold*, viii. 1.
Thuringi, xv. 2.
Ticenum, *Pavia*, vi. 2.
Treveri, *Trier (Treves)*, xxxiii. 5.
Turones, *Tours*, xxxiii. 5.

Vahalis, *the Waal*, xvii. 3.
Vesontio, *Besançon*, xxxiii. 5.
Vienna, xxxiii. 5.
Visula, *the Vistula*, xv. 5.

Wascones, *the Gascons*, v. 2; ix. 2, 3; xv. 3.
Welatabi, xii. 1; xv. 5.
Wilzi, xii. 1.

(b) INDEX OF PERSONAL NAMES

Aaron rex Persarum, xvi. 3.
Adalgisus filius Desiderii, vi. 2, 4.
Adalhaid filia Pippini regis It., xix. 2.
Adallind concubina Caroli Imp., xviii. 3.
Adaltrud filia Caroli Imp., xviii. 3.
Adalungus abbas S. Vedasti, xxxiii. 11.
Albinus, *v.* Alcoinus.
Alcoinus (Albinus), xxv. 2.
Anshelmus comes palatii, ix. 3.
Aragisus dux Beneventanorum, x. 2, 3.
Arn archiepiscopus Salzburgensis, xxxiii. 11.
Atula filia Pippini regis It., xix. 2.
S. Augustinus, xxiv. 2.

Baugulfus abbas Fuldensis, Walahfridi Prol., 2.
Berhta filia Caroli Imp., xviii. 2.
Berhthaid filia Pippini regis It., xix. 2.
Berhtrada mater Caroli Imp., xviii. 4.
Bernhardus rex Italiae, xix. 2.
Bernoinus archiepiscopus Vesontionensis, xxxiii. 11.
Bero comes, xxxiii. 11.
S. Bonifacius, Walahfridi Prol., 2.
Burchardus comes, xxxiii. 11.

Cicero, M. Tullius, Einhardi Prol., 4.

Desiderius rex Langobardorum, vi. 2, 4; xviii. 2, 4.
Drogo filius Caroli Imp., xviii. 3.

Edo comes, xxxiii. 11.
Eggihardus regiae mensae praepositus, ix. 3.

Einhardus, Walahfridi Prol., 1-4; Einhardi Prol., 3.
Engilbertus abbas S. Richarii, xxxiii. 11.
Ercangarius comes, xxxiii. 11.
Ericus dux Foroiulianus, xiii. 4.

Fastrada uxor Caroli Imp., xviii. 3; xx. 3.
Fridugisus abbas S. Bertini, xxxiii. 11.

Geroldus Baioariae praefectus, xiii. 4.
Geroldus comes, xxxiii. 11.
Gersuinda concubina Caroli Imp., xviii. 3.
Gisla filia Caroli Imp., xviii. 2.
Gisla soror Caroli Imp., xviii. 4.
Godofridus rex Danorum, xiv. 2, 3; xxxii. 3.
Grimoldus filius Aragisi, x. 2.
Gundrada filia Pippini regis It., xix. 2.

Hadefonsus Galleciae atque Asturicae rex, xvi. 1.
Hadrianus, Romanae urbis episcopus (pontifex), vi. 1, 4; xix. 3; xxiii. 3.
Haistulfus rex Langobardorum, vi. 1, 2.
Hatto comes, xxxiii. 11.
Heito episcopus Basileensis, xxxiii. 11.
Hildibaldus archiepiscopus Coloniensis, xxxiii. 11.
Hildigarda uxor Caroli Imp., xviii. 2, 4; xxx. 1.
Hildigernus comes, xxxiii. 11.
Hildrichus rex Francorum, i. 1; ii. 1.
Hiltrud filia Caroli Imp., xviii. 3.
Hroccolfus comes, xxxiii. 11.
Hruodgausus Foroiuliani ducatus praefectus, vi. 2.

INDEX OF PERSONAL NAMES

Hruodhaid filia Caroli Imp., xviii. 3.
Hruodlandus Brittanici limitis praefectus, ix. 3.
Hruodtrud, filia Caroli Imp., xviii. 2 ; xix. 2.
Hugus filius Caroli Imp., xviii. 3.
Hunoldus dux Aquitaniae, v. 2.

Iesse, episcopus Ambianensis, xxxiii. 11.
Iohannes archiepiscopus Areliatensis, xxxiii. 11.
Irmino abbas S. Germani Parisiensis, xxxiii. 11.

Karlomannus frater Pippini (III), ii. 3, 4.
Karlomannus filius Pippini (III), iii. 1–4.
Karolus Martellus pater Pippini (III), ii. 2.
Karolus iunior filius Caroli Imp., xiii. 5 ; xviii. 2 ; xix. 2.

Laidradus archiepiscopus Lugdunensis, xxxiii. 11.
Leo pontifex, xxiii. 3 ; xxviii. 1.
Leo Imperator, xvi. 4.
Liutgarda uxor Caroli Imp., xviii. 3.
Ludowicus (Hludowicus) filius Caroli Imp., Imperator, Walahfridi Prol., 3 ; xviii. 2 ; xxx. 1, 2.
Lupus dux Wasconum, v. 2.

Madelgarda concubina Caroli Imp., xviii. 3.
Meginhardus comes, xxxiii. 11.
Meginheri comes, xxxiii. 11.
Michahel Imperator, xvi. 4.

Nicephorus Imperator, xvi. 4.

Otulfus comes, xxxiii. 11.

Petrus Pisanus, xxv. 2.
Pippinus (II) pater Karoli Martelli, ii. 2.
Pippinus (III) pater Karoli Imperatoris, ii. 1 ; iii. 1 ; vi. 1, 2 ; xv. 1.
Pippinus rex Italiae, filius Caroli Imp., vi. 2 ; xiii. 1 ; xviii. 2 ; xix. 2.
Pippinus filius Caroli Imp. ex concubina editus, xx. 1.

Regina concubina Caroli Imp., xviii. 3.
Richolfus archiepiscopus Moguntinus, xxxiii. 11.
Rihwinus comes, xxxiii. 11.
Rumoldus filius Aragisi, x. 2.
Ruothild filia Caroli Imp., xviii. 3.

Stephanus comes, xxxiii. 11.
Stephanus pontifex, i. 1 ; vi. 1.

Tassilo dux Baioariae, xi. 1–4.
Theoderada filia Caroli Imp., xviii. 3.
Theoderada filia Pippini regis It., xix. 2.
Theodericus filius Caroli Imp., xviii. 3.
Theodo filius Tassilonis, xi. 3.
Theodulfus episcopus Aurelianensis, xxxiii. 11.

Unruocus comes, xxxiii. 11.

Waifarius dux Aquitaniae, iii. 1 ; v. 2.
Walah comes, xxxiii. 11.
Walahfridus Strabo (Strabus) Walahfridi Prol., 4.
Waltgaudus episcopus Leodiensis, xxxiii. 11.
Wolfarius archiepiscopus Remensis, xxxiii. 11.

PRINTED IN ENGLAND
AT THE OXFORD UNIVERSITY PRESS